THE CARDINAL MINE

A GHOST OF THE PAST

Signe E. Nakashima

Publisher's Cataloging in Publication
Nakashima, Signe E.
The Cardinal Mine, A Ghost of the Past/
Signe E. Nakashima

Library of Congress Catalog Card Number: 95-92254
ISBN 0-9646928-0-5

1. Mines---Western United States. 2. Names, Geographical---California - Inyo County. 3. The Wilshire-Bishop Creek/Cardinal Mine, History. I. Title.

Cover Art: Ken Stroman

Printed by
CHALFANT PRESS, INC.
450 East Line Street
Bishop, CA 93514
USA

THIS BOOK IS
LOVINGLY DEDICATED
TO
TOSH NAKASHIMA
MY
PATIENT AND SUPPORTIVE
HUSBAND

CONTENTS

PREFACE

This is the history of a mine, one that has been silent and crumbling for fifty-seven years. First known as the Bishop Creek Gold Mine, it underwent complete reorganization in 1906 and became known as the Wilshire/Bishop Creek Mine. In 1933, it came under complete new ownership and was then named the Cardinal Gold Mine.

This book will cover not only the history and operation of the Bishop Creek/Cardinal Gold Mine but include stories of the hard-working people who lived and worked at the mine for its forty-three years of operation. This close-knit community had a true family atmosphere, in spite of (or perhaps because of) the hardships they had to endure. The book also includes history and stories of the town of Laws, the Edison Company, and the road leading up to the mine, as they played a big part in helping to establish and maintain the mine. I could not leave out the village of Aspendell as it is intimately connected with the area.

This year marks the 100th Anniversary of the mine and adjacent village. Much has changed since its beginning but the same family spirit and caring atmosphere still exists. One needs only to step inside the little store and restaurant at the Cardinal Village Resort to feel the friendliness and neighborliness, alive and well today. Or stroll along the dirt road between the cabins or beside the pond to experience the serenity and tranquillity of the area, and feel at peace with the world.

The short walk from the village to the site of the old mine is well worth the effort. One can go there and sit quietly amid the rubble and feel the presence of the ghosts of the hearty men who kept the mine operating for so many years.

In writing this story, I have used original sources

as much as possible, but have taken the liberty to depart somewhat from the original wording in some cases, to make the story smoother and easier to read. I have tried diligently not to change the context of the information presented. At the end of each chapter you will find references to the sources of information which should assist in clarifying any questions that may arise.

I hope you enjoy reading this book as much as I enjoyed writing it.

Signe E. Nakashima

ACKNOWLEDGMENTS

This is the first time I have written a book. I did not realize before, the effort involved or how much fun it would be. I have undertaken this project because I feel the history of this mine must be captured in print while those who remember are still here to tell about it.

Research for this book has taken several years. During this time I have met many wonderful and interesting people, every one extremely warm, friendly and supportive. I consider myself privileged to have met them. They welcomed me into their homes and contributed freely the information and stories they had to share. I have had a great deal of assistance from many fine people and wish to acknowledge them here.

I am especially indebted to Hal and Barbara Cluff of The Cardinal Village Resort who assisted me so much in this work. A special "thank you" goes to Jerry Springer and his mother, Tura Springer, of Pleasant Grove, Utah, for their assistance. I am also truly grateful to Mr. and Mrs. Ernie Kinney of Bishop for their willing and valuable help.

And I must thank the following friends who contributed invaluable information: Mr. Sam Cleland, Mr. and Mrs. Gleason Coen, Mr. Dean Dougherty and his mother, Mrs. Louise Dougherty, Mrs. Maxine Dyer, Mr. and Mrs. G. G. Kieser, Mrs. Lucille Knighton, Mrs. Gebby McMurray, Mr. Raymond Milovich, Mr. and Mrs. Art Schober, Mr. and Mrs. John Schober, Mrs. Dorothy Shultz, and Mr. George Williams, all of Bishop, CA; Mr. Jim Archer, Mr. and Mrs. Jerry Owens, Mr. Ott Sailer, and Mr. and Mrs. Ken Stroman of Aspendell (Bishop) CA; Mr. Mark Allison of Corvallis, OR; Juanita and Rick Apted of the Sabrina Boat Landing; Mr. Neill Olds of Big Pine, CA; Mrs. Florence Ray of Paso Robles, CA; Mr. Larry Stratton of Bend, OR;

Mrs. Loretta Twisselman of Cholome, CA; Mrs. Sandy Williams of Bakersfield, CA; and Dr. and Mrs. David Winkler of Santa Barbara, CA.

Other sources of information have come from the U. S. Forest Service, the Bishop Library, the Laws Railroad Museum, Mr. Richard Kizer of CalTrans, and the Edison Power Company, all of Bishop, CA; the Eastern Sierra Museum, the Inyo County Court House and Library, Independence, CA, as well as other sources too numerous to mention. I appreciate them, one and all.

I wish to sincerely thank Mr. Don Beauregard of Moab, Utah, for his assistance with the first four chapters. Also, I cannot forget my reader and coach, Maryann Butterfield, for her most needed and appreciated assistance. And I appreciate the guidance and encouragement of my professor, Paula Jones, of the Cerro Coso Community College in Ridgecrest, CA.

The cover of this book and the chapter motifs were designed by Mr. Ken Stroman of Aspendell who did a superb job, as usual.

Mr. and Mrs. Bob Ferrey at Chalfant Press in Bishop have been most helpful and cooperative in this effort.

I am happy to take this opportunity to extend a heartfelt "Thank you" to each and every one of you.

Signe E. Nakashima

CHAPTER
I

BISHOP CREEK MINE - THE EARLY DAYS

The Bishop Creek/Cardinal Gold Mine is a thing of the past, a ghost standing silently on the banks of rushing Bishop Creek. The grinding and hammering of the mill and the voices of men at work have been silent for fifty seven years. But its spirit remains. One can stand quietly amid the ruins and feel the presence of those staunch men who worked the mines so long ago.

For centuries the Owens Valley Paiute Indians inhabited the Bishop Creek area. They were hunters and gatherers, and traded goods with the Monache Indians on the western slopes of the Sierra. The white man

1

came into the area in the 1850s and 60s. They started hunting and trapping; then established cattle and sheep camps, followed by logging operations.

During the last half of the 19th century, many mining camps sprang up in California. Eager prospectors searched for gold, silver, and other minerals they expected would make them instantly wealthy. Owens Valley was no exception. The Russ Mining District began mining in 1860 in the Inyo Mountains followed, in 1862, by the Romelia claim, starting the camp of San Carlos. At the same time, the Consort Mining Co. worked claims known as the Golden Wedge north of Laws. More mines quickly followed. In 1863, the Ida and Union mines built some small mills and in 1864, the San Carlos Company started a 5-stamp mill. In 1865, Pablo Flores discovered ore in the Inyo Mountains, northeast of Owens Lake, the controversial beginning of the famous Cerro Gordo mine. Nearer Bishop, some mining was being done in the Paiute District.

In the later part of 1885, prospectors discovered gold on the North Fork of Bishop Creek. This led to the forming of the Bishop Creek Mining District which was recorded in the Inyo County Court House on February 4, 1886. The group unanimously elected Mr. H. A. Man as Mining Recorder. The Mono County line bounded the district on the north, the summit of the White Mountains on the east, Big Pine Creek on the south, and the Sierra foothills on the west.

In 1890, two brothers from Lone Pine, Felix and Charles Meyson, prospecting high in the Sierra, found gold near the headwaters of the Middle Fork of Bishop Creek. They staked a claim and called it the "Tip Top" mine, working it for five years. In 1895, a group of investors from New York City bought the mining rights from the Meysons, calling their company the Bishop Creek Gold Company. And thus began the historical "Bishop Creek Gold Mine."

The property acquired by the new company consisted of a limited mining operation and small tent-village. During the year 1895, the company constructed a small wooden building called the meat-house, the first permanent structure on the property. It was placed in a shady area with a stream running on either side of the building; the surrounding water kept it cool. It was constructed with 16 inch walls filled with sawdust for insulation. That building is still standing today.

Between 1895 and 1905, the company probably did some mining while it was going through various stages of organization. Then on February 16, 1905, an article appeared in the Inyo Register which read, "The 'Bishop Creek Gold Company' has been finally and fully organized in New York City. It is officered as follows: James Gilfillan, President; Col. M. T. Stovall, First Vice President; J. B. Sperry, Secretary. The capitol stock is placed at $5,000,000.00."

The mine is located about 18 miles south west of Bishop in Inyo County, California, at an altitude of approximately 8,500 feet in rugged terrain, surrounded by high mountains. Mt. Emerson, 13,225 feet high, rises on the northwest and 10,500 foot Table Mountain on the east. Further to the southwest lies the Darwin Range including Mt. Lamarck, Mt. Darwin, Mt. Haeckel, and Mt. Gilbert. The mine's location, Bishop Creek Canyon, shows a U-shaped profile, evidence of glacial action.

In the mine area, the maximum temperatures in the summer can reach about 85 degrees F.; temperatures as low as minus 20 degrees F. occur in winter along with a considerable amount of snow fall. Usually about five feet of packed snow covers the area during the cold season.

Today, one would think nothing of driving into Bishop from the mine to go home at the end of a days work. But in the early days it would have taken the better part of a day, over steep and treacherous roads to go into town. In the early 1900s, the only means of transportation was by team and wagon. Consequently, the miners had to have a place to live, close to work. So, the company developed a living area near the mine with bunk houses, cook shack, and a full time cook. For lack of a better name, we will call this area the "village."

During the months of May through July, 1905, the eastern capitalists employed several mine experts to investigate the richness of the ore outcroppings. These outcroppings contained a hard, semitough quartzite ore which was more difficult to fracture than most of the quartzy Mother Lode ores. In May, Col. Winfield Scott Proskey of New York City spent several days at the mine, and in July, Mark B. Kerr, a well known mining expert from San Francisco, along with four assistants, camped for several weeks there. All of them did assay work and research on the mine and were satisfied the lode carried values as had been represented upon the mine's purchase.

The company went through a complete reorganization during the year 1906, with several new officers and directors: James Gilfillan, President; W. B. McReynolds, Vice President; A. A. Hassan (a mineralogist), Consulting Engineer; G. W. Wilkins, Managing Engineer; Paul E. Lodge, Local Agent and Manager, and a very ambitious and visionary fellow named Henry Gaylord Wilshire, a famed and controversial politician, became their Secretary/Treasurer. Along with his enthusiasm, Wilshire brought the wealth he had acquired in the Southern California land boom and began offering stocks for sale at $2.50 a share. He imbued new life into the Bishop Creek Gold Company and began extensive development work which went on for many years. Socialist Gaylord Wilshire and his friends and stockholders, many of whom were socialists also, provided the financing for this work. At this time, too,

4

Wilshire invested in the Tassawini and Aremu gold mines in British Guiana.

The Bishop Creek Gold Company maintained its executive office at 200 William St., New York City, NY, with a local office in Bishop, telephone number, 4930 Beckman. Later, the postal authorities designated the mining camp, "Bishop Creek."

Gaylord Wilshire, being exceptionally enthusiastic about his mine, felt he had one of the finest gold mines ever discovered. In the September 1906 issue of his publication, the *Wilshire Magazine*, he called the Bishop Creek Gold Mine the "World's Greatest Mine" and boasted that the "Tip Top" claim was a "mountain cliff of solid ore."

During the year 1906, the company made many improvements on the property. They built corrals and a stable, three permanent bunkhouses, and three homes for family residences. Men were encouraged to bring their families to the area. The company also built a cook shack and a square, two-story building to be used as the Paymasters Quarters.

The property comprised 33 mining claims and mill site in sections 19, 20, 29, and 30, Township 8 S., Range 31 E. These claims lay generally along the strike of a band of quartzite. They included Sperry Numbers 1 and 2, Comstock, Red Light, Golden Eagle, A. A. Hassan Jr., Mountain Queen, Rocky Point, Sierra Queen, Stovall, the Rising Sun and Wedge Lodes, as well as the Rocky Point mill site. This property encompassed a total of 252.82 acres. Four more claims adjoined the main property: the Wilkins, Tip Top, and Lodge Lodes, and the Mary W. claim. Wilshire filed for a U. S. Government patent on the mine property and received it on February 7, 1910, signed by M. W. Young, Secretary for President William H. Taft.

For the first two years after reorganization, most of the work done on the mine involved exploration of the ore body. In November of 1907, Paul E. Lodge, local agent, telegraphed to Secretary Wilshire in New York that the diamond drill at a depth of 59 feet had encountered ore averaging $17.25 for the last nine feet. This good news encouraged Wilshire to proceed with development of the property.

Labor and equipment costs for the year 1907 totaled approximately $100,000.

Some of the villagers had a successful try at gardening, at least for a time. In the spring of 1908, they planted an experimental vegetable garden, supplying lettuce, onions, radishes, beets and turnips to the entire work force for most of the summer. An extension of the camp water system provided ample water for irrigation. Two Jersey cows, which pastured on land leased from Mr. Pinchot of the Forest Service, furnished fresh milk for the camp all summer, and a flock of chickens and ducks added to the homelike appearance of the place, contributing enough fresh eggs to make them well worth while. In the fall of 1909, the Bishop Creek Gold Mining camp harvested a ton of potatoes for their own use.

No other information could be found on gardens during that era. Several people who lived at the camp during the 1930s stated, "Summers were generally too short and the ground too rocky to make gardening successful." Ground squirrels were also very hard on gardens; as Lou Schober of Bishop puts it, speaking of her flower garden, "The squeakies ate them all!" There are reports of some attempts at gardening being made by the company in the Cardinal era.

By 1908, Wilshire had become president and owner of the company. Convinced that his mining operation required an ore processing capability to be used along with the mining equipment, he decided to build a mill. He then incorporated a separate company, the "Bishop Creek Milling Company," with a capital of

6

$200,000, half of this stock to be held permanently by the Bishop Creek Gold Company.

Sale of the original company's stock had been stopped and the unsold balance, $2,600,000 in shares, remained as treasury stock.

Throughout 1908, building of the 10-stamp mill proceeded. Much of the area near the mine was subject to snow slides, therefore the company built the mill 700 feet from the mine shaft and 50 feet higher. This made it necessary to construct a tramway to transport ore from the mine to ore bins, built behind the mill, to provide a steady stream of rock to the mortars.

The mill's location also placed it on solid granite bed-rock, vitally necessary since the mill employed such heavy stamps. These stamps consisted of 10 pestles, each weighing 1,250 pounds. The pestles were enclosed in a cast-iron mortar, five pestles to a mortar, each mortar weighing about 4 1/2 tons. The foundation for each of these mortars was a block of concrete, each block weighing about 60 tons. Machinery raised the mortars to a height of seven or eight inches, then dropped them onto the ore.

All the heavy timbering used to build the mill was hewn out of whole Lodgepole pine trees with a broad ax. George C. Kinney, whose grandson, Ernest Kinney, lives in Bishop, had the contract as freighter for the mine. He and his teams brought the trees down from the higher elevations in the North Lake area.

Development work continued throughout 1908 which included drilling several diamond-drill holes, driving a double compartment shaft to a depth of 50 feet, and installing a new hoist over it. The main shaft, cut to the 160 foot level with a 60 foot wide crosscut, now produced ore averaging over $15 a ton.

By 1909, the company put a new Leyner drill in service, opened the main shaft to a second level at a depth of 288 feet, and started drifting (horizontal tunneling from the vertical shaft) at this depth. They also began prospecting on the Rising Sun Claim and, further east, on the Mary W. Claim.

Because of the growing activity, many interesting people came into the area. John Schober of Bishop tells this story of one of them. "One of the colorful characters of that era was a man named Mib Hall, known by everyone as 'Old Mib'. He was a likable fellow; the only trouble was, he had a bad drinking problem.

"In 1910, no road led directly from the mine up to Lake Sabrina, so Old Mib was hired by the mine to build one. He proceeded to blast out the boulders and successfully completed a road which was just barely passable by horse and wagon. At one point it was so steep that a team and wagon could go up only with great difficulty. But they couldn't go down because the team could not hold back the wagon; it would literally wipe-out the horses. They solved the problem by driving a steel stake in the ground and winching the wagons down the hill. So they called it 'cable hill'."

"After he completed the road," Schober continued, "Old Mib started prospecting. He found gold right across the canyon from the Bishop Creek Mine. He staked a claim, but soon sold it to the Bishop Creek Company, refusing to accept any money for it. He asked only that they furnish him with enough whiskey to last him the rest of his life. They hauled a truck load of whiskey to his little shack near the Schober Pack Station, not far from the village. He undertook to drink all of it in a couple of days---and it killed him."

As soon as tunneling began in the mine, a problem with water seepage developed and continued to be a problem throughout the life of the mine. The solution necessitated pumping the water out of the shafts, but to do this required electric power.

Early on, the company built a small hydroelectric power plant which used the water coming down the mountain from North Lake. However, expansion of the mine shafts demanded more power than this small plant could produce.

Immediately after becoming involved with the mine, Wilshire filed for water rights on Bishop Creek for mining purposes, at the Inyo County Recorder's Office. In the summer of 1908, he employed a hydraulic engineer to draw plans for a larger and permanent power plant.

In September of 1909, the people of Bishop buzzed with excitement as fifteen tons of machinery from the Sullivan Machinery Company of San Francisco rumbled down main street on its way to the mine. George C. Kinney moved the heavy load from the railroad station at Laws to the mine, a distance of about 20 miles. This required the service of fourteen mules, who pulled the tremendous load in stages up the steep canyon. The machinery consisted of a complete W. J. Sullivan, belt driven power compressor, with one 12' by 48" vertical air receiver which had the capacity for operating nine 3 1/4" slugger type machine drills. The shipment also included a Pelton water wheel, 5 feet in diameter, to be used in the new power plant.

By November the company completed the power plant and put it into operation. They located the new compressor alongside the old one so that in case it was needed, the old one could be brought into service.

Operating a mine at an altitude of 8,500 feet certainly had its drawbacks. In December of 1909, a snow slide took out several sections of the pipe carrying air from the compressor to the hoist, pump and drills, putting that machinery out of business. The damage could have been repaired in a day or two, but four feet of snow over the surface, bad road conditions, and water which nearly filled the mine shaft due to the failure of the pumps, made it too expensive. They decided to leave the water undisturbed until spring.

A short, interesting article appeared in the Owens Valley Herald, which read: "A report has leaked out that the Bishop Creek Mine has water in it. Has anyone ever doubted this from the first?" How true! Water was a constant problem; without pumps running day and night, mining would have been impossible.

On May 10, 1910, headquarters in New York sent word by telegram to pump out the shaft and repair winter damages to the pipe line. Manager Paul Lodge sent a crew of men up to the mine for that purpose. By May 26, after three shifts worked continuously for a week, the mine was completely "unwatered." The crew easily repaired the air main, put the Sullivan air compressor back in order, and made a few minor repairs in the shaft. Most of the men, laid off the previous winter when the mine shut down, returned to work. Drilling began about June 1 at the second level.

After only three weeks of operation, the New York office sent another telegram ordering the shut down of the mine due to an investigation by the U. S. Post Office Department of a stock fraud accusation, involving several hundred thousand dollars.

REFERENCES AND NOTES

Inyo Register: Feb. 4, 1886; June 21, 1894; Feb. 9, 1905; Feb. 16, 1905; May 18, 1905; July 13, 1905; Dec. 28, 1905; July 1908; Feb. 20, 1908; May 28, 1908; Sep. 19, 1908; Oct. 8, 1908; Oct. 22, 1908; Sep. 9, 1909; Nov. 4, 1909; Nov. 25, 1909; Dec. 16, 1909; May 12, 1910; May 26, 1910; June 23, 1910 and Sept. 5, 26, 1906; April 4, 1907; June 20, 1907; Nov. 7, 1907; Jan. 23, 1912.

Owens Valley Herald: June 4, 1909 and Sept. 17, 1909.

U. S. Department of Interior "Information Circular" dated May 1938. "Milling Methods and Costs of the Cardinal Gold Mining Co." written by Walter B. Lenhart.

Wilshire's Magazine, September 1906.

Inyo County Court House, Independence, CA.

Interviews with Gleason Coen, Yan Kinney, Lou Schober and John Schober.

Forbes Photo courtesy Barbara Cluff.

The "Village" in 1914.

Forbes Photo courtesy Los Angeles Historical Society and Eastern California Museum.
Building the Wilshire/Bishop Creek Mill in 1908.

Forbes Photo courtesy Los Angeles Historical Society and Eastern California
        Museum.
The Completed Wilshire/Bishop Creek Mill.

Photo courtesy Laws Railroad Museum.
Three workers ready to go down in the mine. Photo was probably taken between 1900 and 1910. Unfortunately, the names of these men are not known.

Forbes Photo courtesy Los Angeles Historical Society and Eastern
        California Museum.
The main head-frame of the Wilshire/Bishop Creek Mine
looking toward Owens Valley with the Mill in the background.

CHAPTER
II

THE BISHOP CREEK MINE - LATER DAYS

About the third week in June of 1910, the U. S. Post Office Department ordered the Wilshire/Bishop Creek Gold Company to close down the mine, accusing them of stock fraud. Allegedly, Wilshire had used funds raised for another venture to fund the Bishop Creek Mine. Although the charges were unfounded, Wilshire did use profits from the Bishop Creek Gold Company to fund his political ventures, including his unsuccessful bid for Congress on the Socialist Labor ticket.

All mining activities halted, again laying off the complete work force. The company hired Amos Allen as watchman over the mine property during the closure. Gaylord Wilshire proceeded directly from his mines in South America to London, England, to avoid being arrested for stock fraud.

The U. S. Post Office Department conducted a seemingly poorly managed investigation. They sent their inspector, Mr. Booth, to the Bishop area to investigate the case. However, he did not go to the mine, he did not make inquiries of anyone connected with the mine including Manager Paul Lodge; and he did not interrogate anyone at the Inyo County Bank, through which the Wilshire/Bishop Creek Gold Company transacted all its business in Bishop. From "experts who have examined the property," the New York World Herald quotes: "The company claims to own property on the eastern slope of the Sierra Nevada mountains between Tonopah and Goldfield." They further quoted: "The company has developed to the extent of opening cuts, and have some short tunnels," and "Inspector Booth reports that the property now is in about the same state as three years ago."

Those statements revealed what sort of investigation the "quoted experts" and Mr. Booth really made. The mines actually lay at least 80 miles southwest of where the "experts" located them, and in California, not in Nevada. Development had progressed much further than "opening cuts and short tunnels" and they were definitely not "in the same state they were three years ago," by a great deal.

Bishop's postmaster, J. W. Clark, dropped the case when, about the second week in January of 1911, he sent a letter to Mr. Wilshire, expressing complete confidence in the Bishop Creek Mine and stating he believed the extensive improvements on the property indicated the future success of the mine.

During the mine's closure, water again filled the shafts, requiring the lowering of pumps to again unwater the mine. By the middle of July, 1911, after working only three weeks since December of 1909, and being unemployed for over a year and a half, the men finally got their old jobs back. Although Wilshire resided in

Europe, he succeeded in running the operation from London with the help of his manager, Paul Lodge.

During the balance of the year 1911, crews started a second level from the station in the main shaft at the 290 foot depth, using Ingersoll drills. During the year, the company made only a few small shipments of ore. Mining journals reported that ore yielded an average of $8.00 per ton.

In December, heavy snows shut down the mine for the rest of the winter of 1911-12.

Up to this time, the company used the concentration method of processing ore. However, this did not prove successful. Wilshire decided to change to the cyanidation process. In December, he ordered a complete cyanide and amalgamation plant of 50 tons daily capacity from the Colorado Iron Works Co. of Denver. Mr. R. P. Akins, head of the engineering work for that company, and E. W. Walter of Silverton, Colorado, General Superintendent, visited the mine to study the area, take measurements, and insure a speedy installation of the plant when it arrived. A test of ore made at the Colorado Iron Works plant, under the joint supervision of the two men, showed a recovery of 94% of the value in the ore using only 1 1/2 pounds of cyanide per ton of ore, indicating no elements in the ore to interfere with its treatment by the cyanide process.

The mine continued operation throughout 1912 and to the fall of 1913 with only minimal success. In early December a heavy snowfall again closed the mine for the winter.

An article in the Inyo Register dated April 2, 1914, stated, "Ten feet of snow slide covers the road near the mine and resumption of operations must wait its melting away. It will probably be the middle of next month before much can be done. Manager Lodge sent up instructions to have the icy mess blasted to let the air get to it and hasten its removal." This was typical of the many obstacles faced constantly at that elevation.

Early in 1914, at the outbreak of World War I, Gaylord Wilshire returned to the United States, making his home in Los Angeles. He moved the company's headquarters from London to Bishop for greater convenience in transacting business. S. R. Kearns, Vice President of the Bishop Creek Milling Company, arrived in Bishop in February to take charge of the office. In June, Mining Engineer, E. W. Walter, the new Superintendent, arrived to take charge of the active work on the property.

In June of 1914 as in September of 1909, the town's people of Bishop again saw heavy mining equipment rumbling down Main Street. The shipment consisted of the new cyanide plant and amounted to a total of fifty-five tons of equipment. The largest single piece was a sixteen foot tube mill, five feet in diameter, twenty-two feet long over all, and weighing about six tons, quite an imposing piece of freight to be hauled up the steep grade to the mine. An Aking classifier, Portland filter, settling tanks and other accessories made up the remainder of the consignment. By the end of July, wagon freight contractor, George C. Kinney, had delivered all the machinery for the new cyanide plant, from Laws to the mine.

Near the latter part of June, crews at the mine installed a new Starrett pump for the purpose of pumping out the mine-again. Jesse Riley and Ed Green of Bishop assisted in overhauling the compressor and power plant. Jesse Riley (grandfather of Bea McGraw of Bishop) had come from Goldfield, Nevada, with his burros in 1906 to work at the Bishop Creek mine.

Finally, by mid-July, 1914, after being closed for seven months, the mine was unwatered and operational, employing two shifts, developing and blocking out ore in the west drift at the 300 foot level.

George C. Kinney and his teams got the contract

logging out of the North Lake timber country, to supply lumber for the building of the new cyanide plant. The Bishop Creek Gold Company overhauled their sawmill and sawing would begin with the first delivery of logs. They expected to saw out about 100,000 board feet of lumber for the job.

By October of 1914, the logging contractors had brought out over one hundred cords of wood from the North Lake Basin which would keep the plant supplied with fuel for the winter. The sawmill worked full time, completing production of sufficient lumber for the building of the cyanidation plant and another crew of men completed grading for the foundation.

By December, diligent workers finished the new cyanide plant building. Double boarded with paper between for the sake of warmth, it was expected to run continuously through the winter months. By Christmas, the new tube mill was completed, thoroughly tested, and found to be entirely satisfactory. However, due to unfavorable weather conditions, the company deemed it advisable to postpone starting until next spring. Mining operations shut down for the winter.

By May of 1915, the Company had added a new bunkhouse and several new cabins. Mr. Wilshire, president and general manager, also had a comfortable and attractive bungalow built near the approach to the camp where he and his family would make their residence while at the mine. That building no longer exists.

In preparation of restarting operations, in May of 1915, the company installed a big, Gould, electric station pump at the 300 foot level to again unwater the mine. They also installed another Starrett pump, capable of handling all the mine water. The property now had adequate pumping facilities for all its needs.

Also in May, the company completed final assembly and testing of the cyanide and amalgamation plant.

The amalgamation process proved unsuccessful and the plates were replaced by double-deck Deister tables. These tables recovered about 50 percent of the gold, and cyanidation of the tails recovered about 35 percent.

At this time, forty men on two shifts worked in the stopes (tunnels extending horizontally from the main tunnel), moving forward at a very satisfactory pace. Assays showed a little better than $20 a ton for the ore they planned to use at the start in the mill.

During this month, too, H. T. Curran of Colorado took charge as general superintendent, succeeding E. W. Walter, whose private affairs necessitated his return to Colorado; however, Walter would continue to serve the company in a consulting capacity. Also, P. G. Nelson got the freight contract for the coming year.

By October 1, 1915, production from the mine for the year amounted to 5,000 tons of ore which yielded bullion valued at about $55,000. However, even at this level of income, the company could not operate at a profit and Wilshire was running out of money. By the end of October, the mine shut down. A new company called the Consolidated Wilshire Mining Company organized, taking over the stock of the old company on an assessment of six cents a share. The promoters hoped to use this money to double the capacity of the present plant, thus sufficiently reducing the cost per ton, to show a profit. Gaylord Wilshire remained as president of the company, appointing as his officers, John V. Richards, general superintendent, Stuart Elliott his assistant, and Cooper Shapley, general manager.

A tragedy occurred at the mine on October 22, 1915, at 9 a.m. Arthur Joslin, aged about 35, a native of Minnesota and believed to be a single man, lost his life in an accident. He and three other men, McKinsey, Warriner, and Walters, went down in the cage to the 300 foot level to work. Above, Ted Dolan, the top man, dropped the safety gate and ran a loaded car back to dump it. Returning with the empty car, he raised the safety gate and pushed the car forward, ready to be taken down the shaft. It is believed he pushed it too far and it went over into the shaft, breaking up in collision with the sides as it fell. McKinsey, Warriner, and Walters escaped injury but one of the trucks of the broken car struck Joslin in the back of the head, killing him instantly.

Dolan who had been employed by the mine since early July, a very faithful man on excellent terms with all men on the property, and a particularly good friend of Joslins, was nearly overcome with shock and grief when he realized what had happened.

Some of the men took Joslin's body to Bishop by automobile. Justice Yaney, deputy coroner, summoned a jury and held an inquest. Men of the jury were: P. D. Gunter, H. A. Ruble, A. W. Nobles, J. C. Everett, W. G. McCorsky, and J. Wm. Hanby. Ted Dolan went into town and testified at the inquest. The jury reached a verdict of "accidental death." They recommended that the proper officers examine said mine to see that they have proper safety devices for the prevention of such accidents in the future.

Because they could not operate at a profit, the company was finally forced to close the mine. Although it lay idle during the years 1916 to 1919, they did made many improvements to the property. Previous treatment of the ore by the concentration and cyanidation processes had proved unsuccessful. The company decided to try a new method; they added a new flotation plant, changing the flow sheet to the all-flotation process.

They also remodeled the 100-ton concentrating mill and installed a new ball mill. They expected the new mill to take care of between 150 and 170 tons of ore a day. Operations started up in the summer of 1920 and continued until 1922. During that period the plant treated about 27,000 tons, this ore coming from a shallow depth. They achieved a ratio of concentration of about 25 to 1 and a recovery of 90 percent. Ore treated contained $8 to $12 per ton, gold being worth $20.67 per ounce. They shipped concentrates to Midvale, Utah.

The mine did not become the tremendous money making venture Wilshire had expected it to be. By 1922, after investing all of his money into the mine, Gaylord Wilshire was penniless and no longer able to operate his favorite enterprise. Milling operations ceased in February, 1922. Wilshire leased the property to the Consolidated Mining Company who put it in operation on a limited basis until late 1924.

Manny Olds worked for the company during the winter of 1923-24 and throughout the year 1924. He married Faye Neill who worked in the mine office located on E. Line Street just west of the Masonic Temple. Their son, Neill, who now lives in Big Pine, was born in late 1924.

Manny started out as a helper to his brother-in-law, Arch Beauregard who was learning to be an assayer. (Arch Beauregard was married to Elva Olds, sister to Manny Olds). Arch and Manny worked in sampling; that is, they ground ore and assayed it as samples. Later, Manny worked as a helper on the "tables." These big steel shaker tables (averaging 15 feet in length and 8 feet in width) were set at an angle and had riffles on the surface, also angled. Water came onto the table from the top through taps operated by wooden handles. A slushy solution of water and ground rock, came onto the table through a trough or a series of pipes. As the table shook, the gold along with some iron, worked its way to one side where it fell into buckets. After being dumped in a pile to dry, it was sacked and shipped to the smelter.

While working the tables, Mr. Olds realized the richness of the ore, some of the best he had ever seen.

One day the man working with him suggested, "Why don't you and I cut the table?" This meant they could skim off some each day for themselves and make some money on the side. Being a very honest man, Mr. Olds emphatically replied, "No!"

The mine stood idle between 1924 and 28. Every building on the property was locked and displayed a sign "IWW," meaning "Industrial Workers of the World." This was a revolutionary, industrial labor union whose aim was to unite all skilled and unskilled workers for the purpose of overthrowing capitalism and rebuilding society on a socialistic basis.

During the closure of the mine, the company hired a kindly old gent named Mr. Barth to be caretaker. He spent a lot of his time panning for gold in the tailings of the old Bishop Creek Mine.

On September 27, 1927, Henry Gaylord Wilshire died of heart failure in New York City.

A bank in Inyo County took the mine into receivership. The Consolidated Metals Corporation then leased the property. They maintained their office at 752 Mills Building, San Francisco with H. W. Klipstein, Jr., president.

During 1929 and 30, the new company did considerable development work on the property. They worked almost entirely on the Sanford tunnel, which had been driven 400 feet northwesterly on the ore body, with crosscuts at regular intervals. They took about 45,000 tons of ore from this tunnel with an average value of $8 per ton in gold.

In 1931, the company filed in Inyo County Court House, for the Golden Eagle number 4 claim, and in 1933 for Golden Eagle claims, numbers 1, 2, and 3.

From its inception until 1932, the mining company generated its own power, using a Pelton water wheel on the stream coming down from North Lake. The Southern Sierras Power Company wanted the use of that stream; so, they made a trade with the mining company. They ran a power line from Intake II, furnishing power at a very favorable rate to the mine, for the use of the water coming out of North Lake.

Still unable to operate at a profit, the Consolidated Metals Corporation sold out, lock, stock and barrel to the Cardinal Gold Mining Company in October, 1933. The Wilshire/Bishop Creek Mining Company became history.

REFERENCES AND NOTES

Inyo Register: Dec. 15, 1910; Dec. 19, 1910; Jan. 12, 1911; July 27, 1911; Sept. 5, 1912; Feb. 12, 1914; Apr. 2, 1914; May 28, 1914; June 18, 1914; Apr. 30, 1915 and Oct. 28, 1915.

Owens Valley Herald: Dec. 19, 1913; June 26, 1914; July 31, 1914; Oct. 2, 1914; Oct. 23, 1914; Nov. 6, 1914; Nov 14, 1914; Jan. 1, 1915; May 7, 1915; Oct. 28 1915; Nov. 19, 1919 and Apr. 7, 1920.

Seventeenth Report of the State Minerologist, 1920, pp. 281-282.

U. S. Department of Interior "Information Circular" dated May 1938. "Milling Methods and Costs of the Cardinal Gold Mining Co." written by Walter B. Lenhart.

"Mining in California," published monthly by California State Mining Bureau, September 1922, and October 1931.

Conversations and written communications with Don Beauregard. Interviews with Gleason Coen, Ernie and Yan Kinney, Neill Olds, and David Winkler.

Forbes Photo courtesy Los Angeles Historical Society and Eastern
    California Museum.
Head-frame over a mine shaft at the Wilshire/Bishop Creek Mine.

Head frame at the Bishop Creek Mine. The pulley wheel is at the Laws Railroad Museum.

Eastern California Museum Photo.

CHAPTER
III

CARDINAL MINE - A NEW FACE

In October of 1933, the Cardinal Gold Mining Company took possession of the Wilshire Bishop Creek Mine from the Consolidated Metals Corporation, the property consisting of 34 claims, 12 of which were patented. The new company, address 410 Roosevelt Building, Los Angeles, California, hired officers: A. J. Inderrieden, president; Richard H. Travers, vice president; G. Harold Janeway, secretary-treasurer; Victor Bongard, general manager; and Val DeCamp, mining engineer. The latter two men resided in Bishop.

The company sold stocks, one of the principal stock holders being Gene Tunney, the former world heavy-weight champion, who defeated Jack Dempsey in a controversial bout in 1927. Rumors circulated that Slapsy Maxy Rosenbloom, another world champion boxer, also held Cardinal stocks.

The new company made several improvements to the property, one of them being the building of a new hoist house up slope behind the head frame structure. They also did a lot of work underground, developing shafts and drifts to a total length of approximately 4,000 feet with levels at 60, 200, 300, 400, 500 and 600 feet driven from the main shaft. This main shaft went down vertically for the first 100 feet, the remaining 500 feet dropping at an incline. The tunnel at the 200 foot level advanced about 1400 feet, the longest in the Cardinal Mine, extending completely under North Lake.

From the beginning of the settlement until 1933, life at the village varied a great deal, changing with circumstances. Several times the mine shut down, sometimes for more than a year at a time. Families would leave, some would return and others would be replaced by new ones. But because of their remoteness and harsh living conditions, the feeling of "family" always remained.

When the Cardinal Gold Company took over the mine in 1933, the mine and mill ran year round without shut down and life at the village became more stable. The company added many more cabins and a post office/commissary. In the early 1930s, the cook house burned to the ground. The company built an addition onto the paymaster's lodge and moved the cook and his equipment to that building. It remained in use throughout the 1930s. The cook was a fellow named Alvin Scott whom everyone called "Scotty." His wife, Pocohantas, became affectionately known as "Pokey." This very likable couple lived in one section of the paymaster's lodge/cook house building.

In the early 30s, Charles "Charlie" Matlick, who operated a creamery in Bishop, delivered fresh milk, eggs and meat to the camp almost every Saturday. His young daughter, Grace, assisted him in this task. Grace Matlick Wofford now resides in Bishop.

A little one-room school teaching first through eighth grades operated throughout the 1930s. Maxine Scaggs Dyer of Bishop went to school there in her sixth and seventh grades. She vividly remembers her teacher, Margaret Pound.

Cardinal School, 1937.   Maxine Skaggs Dyer Photo.
Standing, left of tree, l to r: Rachel Wallerstead, Maxine Skaggs, Wanda Scott behind Maxine, a Bongard girl in front of Maxine, Billie Oldham in rear, and Barbara Bongard, tilting her head. Standing, right of tree, l to r: John Merrill, Wally ?, and Mrs. Pound. Three unidentified students in front of them. Seated: l to r: Joan: (Swede's daughter), James Ray Oldham, Billy Williams at the back, an unidentified girl in front, Jimmy Piper in the cap, Charles "Junior" ?, and an unidentified girl.
School building in background.

Around 1933 and 1934, the Cardinal Mine operated a delivery truck, a 1933 chain-driven Ford, driven by a fellow named "Three Fingered Red" Hillberg. Tall and thin, he was well-liked by everyone who knew him. He made a trip into Bishop every day, dropping off and picking up mail for the mine and village residents. He also picked up supplies for the mine and for the commissary store and groceries for the cook shack. Villagers also phoned ahead to the store and placed their orders for groceries which he would pick up for them.

At the mine site, the company started the erection of a 150-ton per day, all-flotation mill, scheduled to begin operating on February 15, 1934. However, on February 11 it caught fire and burned to the ground. The company immediately let a contract to erect a new 150-ton capacity mill of fireproof construction, which soon reached completion. Gaylord Wilshire's dream of 20,000 tons per day never materialized.

The mill sent its first shipments of concentrates to Utah to the Midvale plant of the United States Smelting, Refining & Mining Company in August. In the year 1934, the Cardinal Gold Mine produced 50,085 tons of ore, all treated in the 250-ton flotation plant. They shipped concentrates totaling 1,548 tons to the Midvale smelter which in turn, yielded 14,350 ounces of gold and small quantities of silver, copper, and lead.

Although very little need for a law enforcement officer existed at the village, they did hire a constable, Herb Stowe. His duties were more on the order of helper and companion than policeman. Everyone liked and highly respected him and his wife, Elizabeth (Lisa). According to Lou Schober, people would go to Lisa for the 3-Cs; correction, consultation, and comfort. Their son Amos, known as "Aim," worked in the mine.

Some families lived in the company owned

cabins at the village while others lived in Schober's tent cabins located near the Schober Pack station, commonly known as the Pack Shack. These tent cabins, located a short half mile down the road from the village on the west side of Bishop Creek, were regarded as part of the village.

Springer's cabin at Schober's Pack Station.   Springer Photo.

Beryl and Tura Springer lived in one of the tent cabins. Beryl Ott Springer began working at the mine in the summer of 1933, going back to Utah in 1935 to marry his sweetheart, Tura Holm. In 1936, he brought his new bride back to the Cardinal. Tura Springer, who now lives in Pleasant Grove, Utah, describes the tent cabins in this way, "They were small, one or two rooms, but were comfortable and furnished. Most cabins had running water, a sink and electricity. None had an indoor toilet. The kitchen area was adequate, cooking and heating was done with a coal/wood burning stove with an oven (all the housewives insisted on an oven). A wash board, tub and muscle were used to wash clothes. Water for washing clothes and baths was heated on the kitchen stove. Very few people had refrigerators. This was not a problem in winter, of course, Mother Nature provided for that in the High Sierra. In summer an outside cupboard, screened and covered with wet burlap, served the purpose." Tura Springer added, "A detailed description of the cabins in the village would be very similar to that of the tent cabins."

Tura Springer in their 1928 Auburn Convertible Roadster near Bishop.

Springer Photo.

Fred and Millie Merrill and Albert "Sailor" Carlyle and his wife, Laura, (both ladies were sisters of John and Art Schober of Bishop), lived on either side of the Springer's. The same culinary water pipes coming from a nearby spring linked these three cabins together. Pounding on the pipes with a wrench in any of the cabins could be heard in the other two cabins. These three ladies used this as a signal that the coffee pot was hot and to come on over for a cup.

Early on, as a convenience for the workers, the company put in a shower and change room, located in one of the bunkhouses, where the men could clean up before going home after a days work.

Many single workers lived in bunkhouses and took their meals in the mess hall. Beryl Springer's father, J. R. Springer, came down from Utah to work at the mine, living in one of the bunkhouses.

A few employees of the Cardinal built and lived in their own houses in the area now known as Aspendell, a short way down the road from the village. Some of those houses are still used as summer cabins today.

Although the majority of the workers made their homes in and near the village, others lived in several other areas. Some of the workers lived up at a small settlement called Camp Sabrina owned by Angus McMurtrie and his wife, who were friendly, helpful, energetic folks. They went to Bishop once a week to shop for some of the local folks who were not able to get to town. On Friday nights, they took a carload of their neighborhood friends to Keough's Hot Springs to attend the weekly dances.

Located up the road from the village and close to Lake Sabrina on Forest Service land, Camp Sabrina had several houses and a small store stocked with necessary staples, and managed by Ralph and Rosie Domingus during the Cardinal era. The store remained in operation until 1972. The Forest Service finally informed McMurtrie that the houses stood too close to the stream and must be moved back. Since it was not feasible to move them, McMurtire tore down all but one which he sold to Art Schober in October 1974. With the assistance of Jim and Lois Archer of Aspendell, Schober hauled it up the narrow, crooked road to the North Lake pack station, on the back of his truck. Because of the steepness of the grade and the weight of the house, they had to fasten railroad ties to the front bumper of the truck to keep the front wheels from coming off the ground.

That house is still being used today as a bunk house for the cowboys.

Some of the miners lived at another small settlement known as Andrew's Camp, on the South Lake Road, several miles from the mine. Built by Frank Andrews as a tourist retreat, it contained a number of cabins. The miners could purchase their necessary items at a small store at the Schober Lodge, located not too far down the road. After the mine closed, Andrew's Camp stood vacant for several years. Eventually the roofs caved in due to heavy snow loads, and the cabins were torn down. The Four Jeffrey Campground now stands on that site.

Andrew's Camp, 1933.   Springer Photo.

A popular fellow named Jay Selkirk "Kirk" Otey developed a small community west of Bishop, near the present intersection of West Line Street and Red Hill Road. Several workers from the Cardinal chose to live there. The settlement, known as Otey Village, consisted of several houses, Otey's Store, and an airstrip on which Otey kept his own airplane. For years, he enjoyed playing Santa Claus, flying his plane from Otey Village to the Bishop airport where he met the eagerly awaiting children. A short road called "Otey Road" remains as the only reminder of a once active little community.

Some Cardinal employees and their families lived in the town of Bishop, the men commuting to work each day. One fellow who worked for the power company commented, "No one wanted to be on the road during shift change at the mine; those boys would try to break their own speed records coming down the hill!"

Sam Cleland, who still resides in Bishop, was one of the fellows who commuted each day. He worked at the 350 foot level when he was 16 years old. His brother, Deston, "Duke," worked at the mine as a welder. The Cleland boys and another fellow named Bob Brown (who also worked at the mine), car-pooled when they worked on the same shift. Sam still remembers those wild rides up and down the mountain.

The challenging life at the village put everyone "in the same boat," so to speak, and they made do with what they had. Some lived a little better or had nicer cabins and furnishings than others, but all cheerfully helped and looked out for each other. Mining camps were noted for their closeness, helpfulness, and willingness to share what they had in time of need. The Cardinal and Schober camps were like that.

The Cardinal Mine in the Chidago District (previously called the Bishop Creek Mining District) gained the distinction of being recognized as the largest producer of gold ore in the country for the year of 1934.

By 1935, the operation of the mine and mill reached its full capacity. The complete system worked efficiently from mine to smelter. The following is a description written by Mark Allison, of the whole operation, a diagram of which appears on page 40.

A machine called a jaw crusher accomplished the first stage. This consisted of a set of heavy steel jaws, lined with replaceable face plates that had slight, vertical corrugations. The plate was pivoted at the bottom and forced toward the heavy, stationary "jaw" by connecting rods. These rods were driven by a motor and flywheel, similar but in reverse to a steam locomotive's piston-connecting-rod drive-wheel mechanism.

A gyratory crusher made up the next stage in processing. A tall, cast iron cone, it received large chunks of ore at its top. Machinery from the bottom of the cone stirred a long, thick rod in the center. The top end was held in a fixed, pivoting joint. This ingenious arrangement created an increasing diameter of rod movement toward the bottom of the cone allowing the pieces from the larger chunks at the top to be crushed smaller as gravity pulled them toward the bottom, similar in action to a large inverted mortar and pestle.

Conveyer belts fed the crushed ore into a rod mill. This horizontal cylinder, similar to a cement mixer, was kept filled to about one third of its capacity. It contained rods measuring about twelve feet long, four inches in diameter and weighing 350 pounds each. As the cylinder rotated, the rods rolled up the sides and fell on each other crushing the ore even finer. The rod mill was continuously sluiced with water. The "fines," or milky, silty slurry, would be drained off and sent to the flotation tanks. The remaining sand/water mixture, depending on its coarseness, went either directly to the ball mill, or first to the classifier, then the ball mill. Both the ball mill and classifier were sluiced with water to removed the fines.

The classifier was a sloping tank, five feet wide, two feet deep and ten feet long. It processed the coarser sand/water mixture from the rod mill. Inside the classifier were two ladder-like mechanisms that moved in vertical circles in "taffy-puller" fashion. This motion stirred and lifted the water/sand mixture, allowing the fines to be drained off the bottom. The coarser "middlings," or "returns," went to the ball mill.

The ball mill was a rotating cylinder, similar to the rod mill, also oriented horizontally. It was partially filled with iron balls five inches in diameter. The iron balls rolled and dropped on each other, grinding the watery sand into a fine powder. This slurry then went to the flotation tanks.

Box-shaped traps at the ends of both the rod mill and ball mill caught coarse and fine gold as well as other heavy minerals. This was strained to remove small, flattened pieces of free gold, pieces of brass blasting caps, and blasting wire. The material caught in the traps was then put on concentrating tables. These water-filled tanks had horizontally aligned riffles in the bottom. The tanks were shaken, more strongly in the direction of one end, so the material would separate according to each component's specific gravity-gold at one end, light sand at the other. Gold bearing pyrite, pyrrhotite, arsenopyrite, chalcopyrite and sphalerite spread over the grooves between the gold and sand.

Cube-shaped flotation tanks measured three feet on each side. An impeller stirred the fines in the tanks. Pine oil and xanthate were added to the slurry which combined chemically with the gold bearing sulfides and floated to the top of the tank. This frothy emulsion lapped into a trough where it was drained, dried, bagged and shipped to the smelter. In the early days of the Cardinal Mine, these bags were sent to the Selby Smelter in San Francisco. Later they went to the Midvale Smelter in Utah. The smelter heated the sulfide, driving off the sulfur. Chemicals were then added to bind with, and remove other impurities. A glassy slag was formed and removed leaving pure molten gold which was then poured into bullion. This was the finished product.

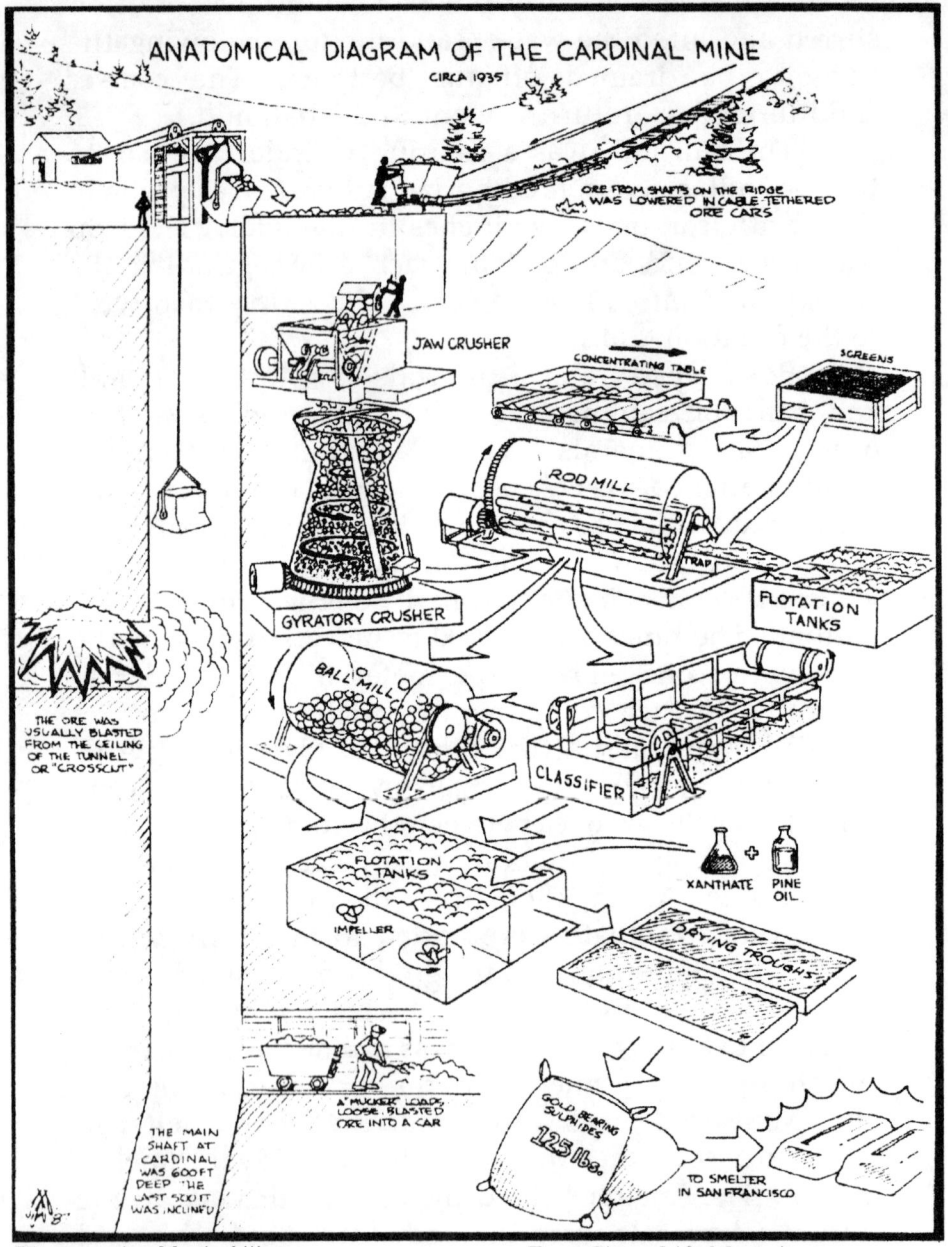

Diagram by Mark Allison.

From Sierra Life Magazine, Sept/Oct 1987.

Beryl O. Springer at the Cardinal in 1933. Springer Photo.

Beryl Ott Springer came to work at the Cardinal in the summer of 1933. Fortunately, he got the opportunity to accompany mining engineer, Val DeCamp, and several others to different parts of California and Nevada, to examine and survey mining prospects the Cardinal Gold Company considered purchasing or leasing. Springer learned the basics of mining engineering and many useful mining skills from DeCamp. Later Springer and his partner, John Eck, worked as "sinkers" for several months. Because of the great amount of underground water accumulating in the lower levels and shaft sumps, a historical fact in this mine, pumps were required. The sinkers drilled shafts using compressed air rock drilling machines and lowered pumps to remove the unwanted water. The drilling machines and the men who operated them were both referred to as "sinkers."

Richard B. Bailey, formerly of Reno, Nevada (now deceased) worked at the Cardinal Mine for several years. He remembered Val DeCamp as a "big, rugged, ruddy-faced, hard-living, hell-raising Dutchman." DeCamp also managed the United Verde Copper Company in

Arizona. According to Bailey, DeCamp would work all day at the copper mine in Arizona, then drive all night to the Cardinal Mine on Bishop Creek. Once there, he would stomp around, raise hell, chew out the foremen and mine workers, sign the checks (in beautiful, almost lady-like handwriting), then drive to Keough's Hot Springs just south of Bishop where he would drink and dance with all the ladies on the outdoor dance floor. Then, at midnight, he would drive back to Arizona!

"DeCamp's 'style' finally killed him," Bailey recalled. "He went to Bolivia to work at the tin mines, carrying on in his usual way at altitudes of 12,000 and 14,000 feet. It finished him off just before he was to get married."

Miners Clyde Russell and John Eck also moved on to South America and Mexico to other mining ventures. Sadly, all three men died at different times and different places in South America.

Bailey also remembered an amusing story about the mill helper's job at the Cardinal Mine. The mill helper had to lift sacks of sulfide powder weighing 125 pounds each. When Bailey arrived at the mine, the job was held by a man of medium build who, by Bailey's calculations, loaded and unloaded about twenty-five tons a day. "These were the days when people didn't just up and quit a job because the work was too hard," Bailey emphasized. "After three or four months of lifting twenty-five tons a day at an elevation of 8,500 feet, the man just plain wore out."

Bailey remembered the man's replacement, ". . . . a big, burly guy. He lasted two months. And then this scrawny kid from Columbia University showed up at the mine and landed the mill helpers job!"

Bailey and the others watched, first with amusement, then with interest, and finally with utter amazement as the kid loaded and unloaded bag after bag, eight hours a day for weeks, and then months! They later learned that before coming to the Cardinal Mine, the kid had spent a considerable amount of time in Bolivia. His high altitude training had served him well.

REFERENCES AND NOTES

The chart of the mine and description of its operation and the stories told by Bailey came from the **Sierra Life Magazine**, Sept/Oct 1987, from the article, **"The Cardinal Mine"** written and illustrated by Mark **Allison.**

U. S. Department of Interior "Information Circular" dated May 1938. "Milling Methods and Costs of the Cardinal Gold Mining Co." written by Walter B. Lenhart.

California Journal of Mines and Geology, October 1938.

Conversations and written communications with Jerry Springer.

Interviews with Jim Archer, Gleason Coen, Hal and Barbara Cluff, Dean Dougherty, Maxine Dyer, Yan Kinney, Ray Milovich, Louise Knighton, John Schober, Lou Schober and David Winkler.

The Cardinal Mill and outbuildings.   Laws Railroad Museum Photo.

Cardinal Mine buildings, including ore bin behind head-frame.

Laws Railroad Museum Photo.

Cardinal Mill showing tailing pond.

Laws Railroad Museum Photo.

CHAPTER
IV

CARDINAL MINE - THE END OF AN ERA

Recreation was an extremely important part of life in so isolated an area. Everyone at the Cardinal Village enjoyed socializing with friends, having them over for dinner or playing cards. On weekends or long shift changes, some families enjoyed traveling to Lake Sabrina, Bishop, June Lake or Mammoth. Or, with their ideal location, they could hike right from their homes into the mountains for a day's outing.

Everyone looked forward to pay day which was a big event. It meant going to Bishop for shopping, a movie, or dinner. On Saturday night, many people would head to Keough's Hot Springs seven miles south of Bishop, a wonderful recreation area in its day. There they could find a dining room and lunch counter, a swimming pool, picnic tables, mineral baths, a bar, and a large, outdoor dance floor. Keough's was a wonderful playground and recreational area for young and old alike.

Several residents loved ice skating, using nearby Intake II, Lake Sabrina and the Pond for their skating rinks. Florence Moncus, an ardent skater, who lived with her husband in the cabin now called Blue Heaven, spent as much time as possible on the ice during the wintertime.

The Cardinal Mine organized a softball team called the "Cardinals," what else? One of their very good, home-run hitters, was none other than "Three Fingered Red" Hillberg. In the summer time, the Cardinals entertained the local folks playing other teams, such as the CCC boys and teams from Bishop and Big Pine.

The men enjoyed another pastime, playing "Pangingi," a game similar to poker. Tables were set up in one corner of the commissary store where signs on the wall read, "Don't spit on the floor" and "Any card you tear will cost you 5 cents." Although popular with the men, the wives felt their husbands were "frittering away their hard earned cash," money that could be used for more useful things.

Maxine Dyer tells a story of her late parents, Elvis C. and Ople Skaggs. Her father worked at the mine as a hoist operator. After one of Elvis' games of Pangini, Ople said emphatically to her husband, "When you go and P. A. N., I'm going to C. O. D.!" And she did. She would get out the catalog and make out an order (only for items they needed) for about the same amount of

Ople Skaggs.   Maxine Dyer Photo.

money he spent playing P. A. N.!

Lucille Knighton of Bishop tells another tale of Pangingi. She and her late husband, Leuis (Lou), rented a cabin at the village while building a small cottage, just down the road from the post office / commissary. They did all the work by themselves including clearing away the rocks and doing the actual construction work. Lou worked as a contractor in the main shaft of the mine during the years 1935 and 1936.

One afternoon he called her and said he had to work overtime. A little later, a neighbor informed her that he was actually in the store, playing Pangingi! She became very angry; he was wasting the money they were saving to build their house! She began to clear their property of rocks, by hand. A neighbor came by and asked, "Can I help you? Those rocks are too heavy for you to lift."

"No! That's okay!" Lucille snapped. "I'm mad at my husband!"

The Cardinal wives shared this typical feeling toward the game of Pangingi.

The Knightons left the Cardinal in late 1936 and moved into Bishop. The Schobers purchased their little dream house and moved it to the pack station at North Lake where it became a bunk house for the cowboys. An avalanche in 1968 totally demolished the building. It was finally replaced by the one Art Schober hauled up from Camp Sabrina in 1974.

A second tragedy occurred at the mine on July 8, 1935. A worker in the mill, Percy Herbert Pinneo, known to all acquaintances as "Bert," lost his life in an accident.

Shiftboss, Charles A. Green noticed leaks at the ends of two or three of the liner bolts of the rod mill and directed operator Fred C. Fellmuth to shut down the mill while repairs were being made. This did not take long, and before the mill started again, Green and mill superintendent Wallerstedt tightened up two manhole bolts. Pinneo had assisted in the work, and had climbed into the ball mill to put new bolts through to the outside. Fellmuth went upstairs for some brief purpose, and on descending saw Pinneo and Wallerstedt standing together. Green, knowing that the work for which the stoppage had been made, had been finished, said, "Let's go," and Fellmuth threw the switch which started the rod mill. Wallerstedt, who had stepped away, heard a cry and signaled for a stop.

For some reason which no one could guess, Pinneo had climbed back into the rod mill, unknown to the others. A revolution, the only one between the starting and stopping, crushed him under the dropping rods. These rods, weighing about 260 pounds each, make an aggregate mass of about twelve tons which tumble as the big cylinder turns.

The men summoned Dr. Anderson but nothing could be done as Pinneo must have died instantly as the masses of iron fell on him.

Acting Coroner Patterson held an inquest with Marvin Lutzow, Robert Dean, Nick Pappas, Harry Caffrey, Ward Bodle, Frank Matlick, H. A. VanLoon, Juel Thompson, Claude Shepherd, Harold Bush, Wayne E. French, and J. M. Reynolds as jurors. After hearing the evidence of Dr. Anderson, G. A. Wallerstedt, Charles Green, Roy Vonde, Fred C. Fellmuth, and Deston Cleland, they returned a verdict of accidental death.

Twenty four-year old Bert Pinneo, a native of Manning, Utah, had been one of the most popular men in the camp. He had worked at the mill since the previous September and had been married only a few months before his death.

In the mine's 43 years of operation, only two deaths by accident occurred; not a bad record considering the dangers involved in the mining occupation.

In 1936, the principal mining operation for the year in the Chidago District was the Cardinal Gold Mine. They reported an operating profit of $81,532 for the first four months of the year, as compared with $55,446 for the same period last year. The company distributed $100,000 in dividends during the year.

By the winter of 1936-37, the mine operated at its peak, their ample electric power contributed greatly to their success. The two powerful Sullivan air compressors and the numerous Ingersoll compressed air rock drilling machines the company had earlier installed were also major contributing factors.

Village life continued in its friendly, energetic and efficient manner. In late spring and summer, residents went into Bishop once a week to buy their week's supply of groceries, usually getting them from the Safeway store. As an example of food costs in 1937, the Bishop Safeway store sold a 40 oz. package of Bisquick for 29 cents, two pounds of brown sugar for 15 cents, local large eggs for 30 cents a dozen and butter for 37 cents a pound. In the fall, everyone stocked up on vegetables such as potatoes, carrots and dried beans, canned goods, flour, sugar, coffee, rice and other staples, enough to last for a couple of months. In the wintertime, typical meals were meat and potatoes, stews, soups, and chili.

Residents never knew when heavy snow would cover the area, leaving them isolated for a month or more at a time. During the winter, highway crews cleared the road as far up as Plant 4, where the villagers left their cars. To go into Bishop for supplies, they walked or rode their sleds or toboggans down to Plant 4. On their return, they walked the approximately eight miles back home, pulling their sleds with loads tied on.

The winter of 1936-37 saw a near record snow pack and terribly cold temperatures. In January, the temperature hit a low of minus 14 degrees F. That winter lasted well into late spring.

Yan Kinney's mother, Mrs. Lenhart, had a nice flower garden growing in front of her cabin (now called Emerald Cabin.) In mid-June it started snowing. Mrs. Lenhart rushed out and covered her flowers with cans to prevent them from freezing. When it quit snowing, her front yard looked like a miniature cemetery with little tombstones standing in neat order.

The Lenhart's home at the Village.   Yan Kinney Photo.

In the year 1937, the executive personnel of the Cardinal Gold Mining Co., remained the same as in 1933, when the company took possession of the mine. At this time, the company employed the following supervising personnel: Walter B. Lenhart (father of Yan Kinney of Bishop), Mill Superintendent; A. B. Weston, Mine Superintendent; Charles Green, Master Mechanic; J. C. B. Amos, Purchasing Agent and Auditor; Charles F. Johnson, Mining Engineer; J. Denman Jones, Assayer; and a Mr. Amos, bookkeeper.

Personnel employed by the Cardinal Gold Company varied to some extent through the years of operation; however, it remained very similar to the following description of the 1937 crew. One operator and a helper on each shift looked after the entire milling operation. The day-shift helper assisted in sacking the concentrates; the afternoon helper washed the mill floor, brought in the 24-hour supply of Portland cement, prepared the reagents, cleaned sample buckets, and attended to other details. The graveyard shift helper did all the greasing and oiling, except of the electrical equipment which was done by an electrician's helper. One man sacked concentrates and assisted in handling table products. A total of 10 men, including the three tailing-pond attendants, were under the direction of the mill superintendent. The day operator acted as foreman.

The above listed operating crew made all routine repairs which included changing leaves on the filter, tightening liner bolts, changing pump runners and repairing pumps and flotation equipment. The repair gang that served the mine and surface workings under the direction of the master mechanic made any other repairs necessary.

The surface crew comprised about twelve men, charging their work each day to the mill, camp or mine. This crew consisted of one each: carpenter, electrician, electrician's helper, welder, repairman, truck driver, and caterpillar operator. It also included three men in the machine shop and three on the "bull" gang.

In addition, four men in the steel shop who sharpened and repaired mine steel, a drill "doctor," and a compressor operator made up one shift. The drill "doctor" and one of the machine shop men looked after the compressors on the other two shifts.

The mine layout comprised a mill, crusher building, compressor and machine shop building, drillsteel shop, hoist house, oil-storage building, an assay office, and administrative offices.

The mill, including the crushing plant, was of steel construction, covered with corrugated iron. The interiors of the buildings were lined with gypsum wallboard making it quite comfortable within, during the coldest weather. The bins were made of wood.

The compressor and machine shop building housed two class WN-3, Sullivan, angle, compound compressors, each having a capacity of 1,340 cubic feet per minute, that delivered air to the mine. One of the compressors was driven by a "V" belt drive and the other by an endless leather belt. The machine shop section consisted of a 20- and a 15-inch lathe, shaper, power hacksaw, drill presses, and other smaller equipment, making this a very complete shop.

The assay office contained two type 1111, Denver fireclay muffle furnaces, the usual crushing and grinding equipment and core splitter, filters, and electric dryers. One assayer and one helper assayed on an average, about 15 mill samples and 30 mine samples each day, running a maximum of about 90 per day. Gold was the only metal determined although the assay office was also equipped with materials for making practically all of the ordinary wet, nonmetallic, and metallic determinations.

Mine equipment included: an electric hoist; two motor driven, Sullivan air compressors having a combined capacity of 2,340 cubic feet per minute; numerous Ingersoll compressed air, rock drilling machines; complete blacksmith shop with Sullivan drill sharpener and automatic (hot lead) tempering machine; carpenter shop; machine shop; and assay office. Two sinking pumps and a three inch centrifugal pump handled water to the 300 foot level where a 350 gallon per minute triplex pump boosted it to the surface.

During its last eight months of operation, the Cardinal Mine, considered one of the ten leading producers of gold ore in California, yielded 536 pounds of gold, 155 pounds of silver and 4,395 pounds of copper.

The Cardinal Gold Mining Company ceased operations on August 29, 1938. One hundred five men (approximately 40 of those working underground) were employed at the time. Opinions vary on the reason for closure. Some say that, due to the war effort, men were not available to continue working the mine. Another and more widely accepted opinion: no new ore was found; they just ran out of gold-bearing ore. The speculation that the Cardinal might reopen as a tungsten producer never materialized.

In its total time of operation, the Wilshire Bishop Creek/Cardinal Gold Mine had produced approximately $1,600,000 in gold.

As a summary of the Bishop Creek/Cardinal Gold Mine: the management, being always exceptionally safety conscious made it an extremely safe mine. The company continually updated its equipment and machines with some of the best found in the industry. It kept good working conditions and paid its employees better than the average wage, especially considering the fact that the whole country had gone through a major, national depression. And as frosting on the cake, the mine and living area was situated in a scenic, almost resort like, mountain area. The overall consensus: "It was a great place to be employed!"

When the mine closed its doors, the village became a ghost town. The miners and their families all went their separate ways. Some of them went to other towns and other mines; some went back to their home states.

Herb Stowe, the constable, went to work for the Nevada-California Electric Corp., the power company on Bishop Creek. At times he stayed at Intake II in the winter and Lake Sabrina in the summer months. The Springer family had already moved back to Utah. Elvis and Ople Skaggs went to Pine Creek to the vanadium mine for awhile, then moved on to Bodie, California. The Moncus family moved on; Florence now lives in Paso Robles, California. And "Three Fingered Red" went to work at the vanadium mine up Pine Creek.

The friendly, close-knit, family feeling and respectful regard for each other that flourished in the unique community of the Cardinal Village and its nearby sites, lives on in the memories of those remaining who had the privilege of living there. This feeling can still be found today at the "new village," the Cardinal Resort.

Walter B. Lenhart, Mill Superintendent, on the left.
Victor Bongard, Mining Engineer, on the right.

Walter Lenhart, left, and Victor Bongard, right, in front of the
Bongard's home.   Both are Yan Kinney Photos.

Elvis C. Skaggs, Maxine Dyer's father and hoist operator at the Cardinal.

Maxine Dyer Photo.

Ira Noble, father of Ople Skaggs. He was the tailing pond operator.

Maxine Dyer Photo.

Beryl Springer's engineering tools which he used at the Cardinal Mine. They include a carbide lamp, Brunton, mineral glass, watch and the all-important pocket knife.

Springer Photo.

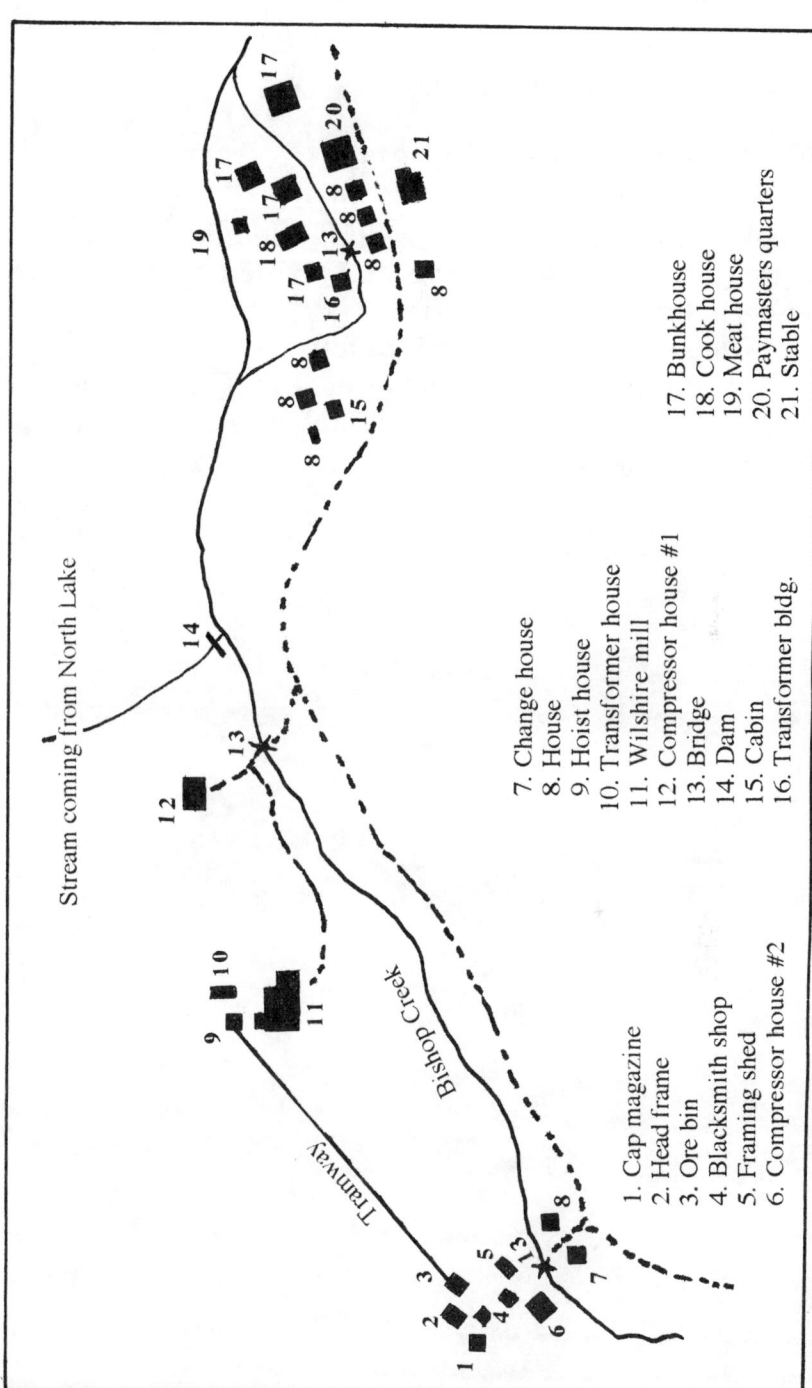

Map of the Village and Rocky Point Mill Site as it appeared in 1920.

1. Cap magazine
2. Head frame
3. Ore bin
4. Blacksmith shop
5. Framing shed
6. Compressor house #2
7. Change house
8. House
9. Hoist house
10. Transformer house
11. Wilshire mill
12. Compressor house #1
13. Bridge
14. Dam
15. Cabin
16. Transformer bldg.
17. Bunkhouse
18. Cook house
19. Meat house
20. Paymasters quarters
21. Stable

Stream coming from North Lake

Tramway

Bishop Creek

Taken from a 1920 map belonging to Larry Stratton.

REFERENCES AND NOTES

Inyo Register: July 11, 1935.

U. S. Department of Interior "Information Circular" dated May 1938. "Milling Methods and Costs of the Cardinal Gold Mining Co." written by Walter B. Lenhart.

Map courtesy of Larry Stratton.

Interviews with Maxine Dyer, Yan Kinney, Lucille Knighton, Florence Ray, Lou Schober, Jerry Springer, and David Winkler.

CHAPTER V

THE OLD COACH ROAD

There's hardly a wheel rut left to show
The way the coach road used to go.
Trees straddle it and bushes grow,
Where coaches rumbled long ago,
And horses' hoofs struck sparks of light,
Many a frosty winter night.
Here miner's faces, lean and tan,
Peered from some lumbering caravan,
Or packers passed with bulging packs,
And mules with sun aslant their backs.
Now, only fishing people push
Their way through thorn and elder bush.
But sometimes of a night they say,
Wheels have been heard to pass this way.

Author Unknown

Before the Bishop Creek road existed, Indians living in the canyon, used trails leading up along the creek, past North Lake and on over Paiute Pass. In the latter half of the nineteenth century lumber men built a one-way, dirt road to provide access to the Sabrina and North Lake areas. Miners probably improved it somewhat when they began operations up Bishop Creek Canyon in the 1890s.

In early 1905, the Nevada Power, Mining & Milling Co. began developing power plants along Bishop Creek. Supervised by a Mr. Lund, the company built a road from Bishop to Plant 2 spending over $40,000 total on the project. Starting in Bishop, this wagon road led into the canyon past a solitary pine tree, visible from the valley. It then proceeded up the north side of the creek. The first two mile section, with a 10 percent grade and costing $3,500 a mile, was carved along the north wall of the canyon to the broader area, the present location of Plant 3. From there to Plant 2, the road followed along the creek, having a moderate to heavy grade all the way. The Bishop Creek Gold Mining Company aided to some extent in the building of the road as they were also going to use it.

The road from Plant 2 switch-backed up a steep grade past Intake II and eventually arrived at the mine area, staying on the west side of the Bishop Creek all the way to the mine. There are still signs of the old road here and there along the way.

According to CalTrans records, a narrow, one-way wagon road originally went west of Bishop, up through Sand Canyon, then over a ridge, joining the Bishop Creek road near Plant 3. Even as late as April 1953, a CalTrans Project Report described this road in the following way: ". . . the present facility is an old country road, unsurveyed and laid on a route of least resistance down between the boulders." That pretty well describes the road's condition the entire time the Cardinal residents used it to go to town for supplies, and the mining and power companys, to haul tons of heavy equipment up to their locations.

From Bishop, miners could use either the Bishop Creek or the Sand Canyon route. Many cars used the Bishop Creek road, however, it was too narrow and crooked to haul heavy equipment up to the mine. All the freighters had to use the road up Sand Canyon. Many autos used this road, as well.

Gaylord Wilshire wrote the following story in 1906 which describes quite well a trip up to the mine in the early days, using the Sand Canyon route.

"Put a big sombrero on your head. It is comfortable and you look picturesque. Get into that seat in this buckboard and we'll drive out of the embowered town of Bishop and up to the 'Park' in the Sierras. Everybody hereabouts goes there in the summer time.

"For nearly four miles westward we drive through a lane bordered and shaded by trees. It is a good road. At the end of this our climb begins and the road becomes heavier. Two hours' drive on the heavy, uphill grade to the head of a dry canyon. We look backward. Lo, the valley has dwarfed to a ribbon of varied green, mottled with gray, the White Mountains loom in the East twice higher than they seem from the town.

"The mournful roaring which you begin to note, inquiringly, is not the voice of a tempest through the gorges and pines; but the angry bellowing of a torrent, hurrying out of a score or more of pretty lakelets and fresh water seas far up in the exalted reaches of that enormous uplift, the slope of which we are climbing. Passing a 'divide' we reach the main canyon whence the roaring comes. Up and beside its violent waters we must continue in order to reach the Park which we seek. For three more hours the toiling horses take us up, steadily upward, through the canyon, along the banks of this vociferous stream.

"Now, at an altitude of 8,000 feet the Park Gates open and here we are in one of the loveliest spots on the globe, a green-carpeted vale illuminated with flowers. Bunch grasses of the hills border the clover and flowers and fruiting vines of this little summer paradise."

Route 76, 12.43 miles west of Bishop.   CalTrans Photo.

In October of 1914, a group of people from the State Highway Commission, escorting Governor Hiram W. Johnson through California, made a trip up the road to the Bishop Creek Mine, doing research on establishing State Highways.

The State of California finally took the Bishop Creek road into the State Highway System from Inyo

County on August 22, 1933, giving it the designation, "Route 76." According to the CalTrans report, all the roads taken into the system at that time were "dirt or gravel with no particular standards." In 1964, the state renamed the road, "State Highway 168."

In 1934, the Highway Department applied an oil penetration treatment which improved the road conditions a great deal. In 1938 and again in 1941, they widened and surfaced the roadway from Otey Village into town. The rest of the highway from Otey Village to the mine remained essentially the same from about 1938 to 1965. A few minor improvements were made, but nothing to change the character of the highway. Then in 1965, a realignment project changed the road to its present location from about Shepard Lane to above Edison's Plant 3. In 1966, another project realigned the road from above Plant 3 to Aspendell and in 1967, from Aspendell to the end of the highway near the North Lake turnoff.

This road remained a "one-way road with turn-outs" during the mining days, from the mine's beginning to its closure in 1938. On this type of road when two vehicles met, someone had to give the right-of-way, the rule being, "down hill traffic must yield right-of-way to uphill vehicles." Old timers who traveled the road remember, "When we met a new comer to the area, whether going up or down, the new comer was usually too frightened to back up; it was up to us who were familiar with the road to do the backing up." Backing up anywhere on this very narrow road was quite a terrifying experience. The seventeen mile trip from Bishop to the mine, a rise in elevation of some 4,500 feet, was an arduous journey, described by the old-timers in various ways; scary, terrifying, dangerous and a "long, hard grind." One old fellow said, "You just ground along in first or second gear, all the way." And most people do not forget the BIG switch back!

Automobile waiting at a turnout,   CalTrans Photo.
   7.73 miles west of Bishop.

During the winter, the highway crews cleared the
road of snow as far up as Plant 4 where the villagers left
their cars and went the rest of the way on foot, pulling
their sleds. In summer drivers stopped in the same
area, to let their radiators cool and add more water. It
was not at all uncommon in the summertime for cars
to vapor lock coming up the steep grade. In the early
days, before the advent of the automobile, miners
stopped in this same area to feed and water their horses.

In October, 1967, the local Division of Highways
received authorization from John A. Legarra, state
highway engineer, to clear snow from Highway 168 all
the way to Aspendell. To the date of this writing, the
road from Aspendell to Lake Sabrina still remains
closed all winter.

It is hard to imagine now, driving from Bishop to
the mine area in about 20 minutes, sailing along on a

smooth, black-top highway, what the road must have been like in the early days. As an example, quoting from an Owens Valley Herald article of May 29, 1914: "Gaylord Wilshire arrived in Bishop last Friday for a visit to the property. The trip to the mine was made easily in one of the new Ford cars from the Leece and Watterson garage, A. M. Shiveley driving, in 2 hours and 45 minutes, from Bishop to the camp. This was considered very satisfactory for a car that was new and stiff. The road is in the best shape it has been in a long time."

An interesting event happened in July of that same year. The following article appeared in the Owens Valley Herald dated July 31, 1914.

"By driving his machine up 'Cable Hill' near the Bishop Creek Mine, U. G. Smith on Thursday, settled an argument of long standing regarding the pull-power of two local cars. Mr. Smith drove a Buick "30" made in 1910. Alex Reeve, driving Bud Lily's Buick "Twenty," attempted to follow Smith up the hill but failed.

"The old "30" has been the pride of the Pasear garage of which Mr. Smith and Irl Newlan have been the proprietors for the past four years. Both men have often made the assertion that it could out-pull any car in the county. The performances of the car have given force to the assertion, so much force that no one has felt inclined to dispute it---except Lily. That gentleman disputed it so often and so emphatically that one of the most unique contests ever pulled off in this state resulted.

"According to the rules of the contest, Alex Reeve, driving Lily's car, was to follow Smith from 7 A.M. to sundown over any route the automobile dealer saw fit to travel, the cars not to run over 15 miles per hour and the total distance to be covered in the day's run not to exceed 75 miles. Reeve could take as much time as he needed to duplicate the feats of the leading Buick but must be up with it at sundown to win the contest.

"The first test by Smith was a bit of deep sand on the road running from the Warm Springs school house to Butler Lane. Alex followed through this without difficulty. They then ran to the Hiram Smith ranch. At that point, Smith drove his car up the side of a steep hill through sage brush and over rocks and loose gravel. Reeve was close behind when he reached the top. The grade on this hill was about 22 percent. The next stunt tackled was the climb up the road from Bishop to the Bishop Creek Mine. Both cars made the trip, although the little Buick had some difficulty in negotiating the heavy grade.

"Then came the final test, the climb up Cable Hill. The grade here is between 35 and 40 percent. There is practically no road except a track made by wagons which were winched down by cable. This track is exceedingly rough and rocky. It was against the rules of the contest to remove these rocks. The hill is about 600 feet long. Smith made the ascent in exactly eighteen minutes. When he reached the top, Alex Reeve, driving the Lily car, attempted the climb. The little car made a noble effort but her engine failed to develop sufficient power to reach the top.

"The judges were Ed. McNamee, Walter Utter and Jake Hodge. Several hundred dollars changed hands as a result of the contest."

One winter in the early 1930s, during a lull in work at the mine, three of the miners decided to walk down to their parked car and drive into town for a day of relaxation. After partaking a little too much of "a bit of the bubbly," they drove back to the parking area. Seeing a snow bank, one of the fellows challenged the other two to a contest; each was to stick his head into the snow; the one who stayed the longest would receive 50 cents from each of the other two. The first man put his head into the snow, stayed a short time, then came up for air. The second man did the same staying a bit longer than the first. The third contestant thrust his head into the drift and remained motionless for some time. Becoming worried, the other two finally pulled him from the drift; he was unconscious and bleeding. He had, in his desire to outdo the rest, plunged in too enthusiastically, hitting a rock and cutting his head. One of the fellows walked up to the village where he contacted Constable Herb Stowe. Returning to the injured man with a sled, they tied him on the vehicle. After taking him home over the snow drifts, he recovered with no lasting ill effects. No doubt he collected 50 cents from each of his fellow opponents.

The road was the lifeline between the Cardinal and the town of Bishop, the only route in and out of the mine area. Everything and everyone in the upper Bishop Creek area had to come in on that road. Many tales were told about the adventures over this narrow, twisting trail. The following are two such adventures.

Jerry Springer of Pleasant Grove, Utah, was born on January 21, 1937. His mother, Tura, recalls: "We were living in a tent cabin near the Schober Pack Shack. Because of the heavy snow and near record cold temperatures, arrangements were made for me to board in Bishop with my friend, Merle Rose, just prior to my son's birth. When the time came to be driven to the hospital, two different neighbors of Merle's tried but could not get their cars started. It was quite difficult, as big as I was, to keep getting in and out of those cars. It became very funny; in fact, by the time I got in the third car, I was laughing so hard, I had tears in my eyes. A very helpful manager of the Clark Williams Hospital was called; he was able to come and get me." Tura was the only patient in the hospital for several days; the next patient was a Cardinal miner and friend of Tura's, who had developed pneumonia.

The Springers with their new son, drove back up "the hill" to their tent cabin on February 2. Even with tire chains, the road was just barely passable. The Cardinal Company, concerned about their safety, sent a snow plow and crew part way down to clear a path and tow the car back to the camp. Those two vehicles were the last to travel the canyon until February 15.

When they arrived at their tent cabin home, Beryl Springer and some of his friends had to dig a snow trench and tunnel over six feet high and more than thirty feet long from the road to the cabin door.

Snowplow clearing the Bishop Creek Road in the 1930s.   CalTrans Photo.

During the same winter of 1937, Ray and Florence Moncus (now Florence Ray) lived in the building now known as Blue Heaven cabin. Florence was expecting a baby in April. She awoke the morning of February 15, not feeling well and realizing about mid-morning that she had started labor prematurely. She was frightened and had not the slightest idea what to do. After what seemed an eternity, one of the miner's wives stopped by, seeming to Florence like an "angel from heaven." The lady immediately went for help and the excitement began. The rest of the miner's wives congregated in Florence's cabin, discussing their unforgettable moments in childbirth and various plans for delivering Florence's baby.

The Cardinal Gold Company gave ten of their employees the day off to devise a way of transporting Florence to the hospital in Bishop, seventeen miles away. These ingenious men constructed a sled and hitched it to a Caterpillar tractor. They telephoned the hospital in Bishop, then contacted the highway department who quickly dispatched a snow plow, followed by an ambulance, in the direction of Cardinal Village. The immense storm had completely closed the road all the way from Bishop to the mine. Several miners had gone into Bishop just before the storm and could not return home. When they heard a snow plow was making its way toward the mine, they all followed.

Meanwhile, back at the village, the men bundled Florence onto the sled and with several men on foot and a woman to assist should they lose the race with the stork, began their arduous journey down the mountain. The "Big Cat," operated by Carl Cleland and his sons, Sam and Duke, rambled and roared over deep snowdrifts. After nine miles of fear and discomfort, they met the contingent from Bishop.

Because of the tremendous amount of snow the ambulance was unable to turn around, but this did not discourage those capable men. The group of fellows who had been following the ambulance, physically picked it up and turned it around. Florence was transferred from sled to ambulance and with sirens screaming, they raced down the steep hillside, reaching the Clark Williams Hospital at Elm and Home Street in record time. A short time later, Dr. Charles Anderson delivered a healthy, active 4 1/2 pound baby girl, Loretta Ray.

Senator Keough who was in the hospital at the time, soon took over the "duties" of showing "Little Miss Snowball," as she was immediately nicknamed, to everyone who came into the hospital.

Still healthy and active today, Loretta lives with her husband on a 20,000 acre cattle ranch near Cholome, California. Florence, too, is still healthy and active. She recalls with a smile and a twinkle in her eyes, her wild ride down the mountain side, 58 years ago.

But that is not the end of the story!

The Cardinal Gold Company had put Walter B. Lenhart (father of Yan Kinney of Bishop), Mill Superintendent of the mine and a very talented and capable man, in charge of building the sled. Lenhart, Lou Knighton and several other men, accompanied the sled to see that everything went well. They returned home, wet and cold; in fact, they were chilled to the bone. From this, Mr. Lenhart caught a cold which turned into pneumonia, putting him in the hospital, the same one in which Little Miss Snowball was born. He was hospitalized for several days.

While there, his ex-wife, Ann, from whom he had been divorced for several years, came to visit him. They reconciled, fell in love all over again, remarried and lived happily ever after!

Upon Little Miss Snowball's arrival, Gebby (now Gebby McMurray of Bishop), Florence's sister, felt terrible because she had not received her paycheck in time to buy a gift for her niece. Mrs. Lenhart, a close friend of Florence, purchased a nice zippered-bunting for Gebby to give to Loretta. To show her appreciation, Gebby did many nice things for Yan and her sisters. As they grew older, Gebby introduced Yan to Ernest Kinney, giving her stamp of approval on him. As a result, Yan and Ernest were married; and they too, have lived happily ever after!

After Mr. and Mrs. Lenhart reunited, they moved to a building, now called Emerald cabin, at the Cardinal Village. The nearest high school which Yan and her sister, Rose, could attend was in Bishop. Because of the distance and road conditions, the girls could not commute daily to school. They found homes in Bishop where they received their room and board during the week, coming home only on the weekends.

Some of the old road along Bishop Creek between Plants 4 and 5 is still visible and even in use, for a ways. It remains just as narrow with the old "turn out" signs still in place. The old road going up through Sand Canyon over the ridge is still passable but only with a 4-wheel drive vehicle.

Today, State Highway 168 is a modern highway, a scenic and historic road. The greatest hazards would probably be deer crossing the roadway in spring, summer and autumn; and spots of "black ice" (which can be a very unpleasant surprise) in the winter time.

REFERENCES AND NOTES

Inyo Register: Apr. 25, 1907; May 28, 1914; Oct. 19, 1967. Owens Valley Herald: May 29, 1914; July 31, 1914; Oct. 2, 1914.

"Notes on History of Hwy. 168, Bishop to Lake Sabrina" from Richard Kizer, CalTrans, Bishop, CA.

Wilshire's Magazine, September 1906.

Interviews with Gleason Coen, Gebby McMurray, Florence Ray, John Schober, Lou Schober, Jerry Springer and Loretta Twissleman.

Blasting to clear the highway between
the Village and Lake Sabrina. Photo is
looking toward Owens Valley.

CalTrans Photo.

The road in the early 1930s.

CalTrans Photo.

CHAPTER
VI

LAWS AND THE RAILROAD MUSEUM

It was an exciting day that April first in 1883. A train rolled into a little settlement called "Station" for the first time ever. This would become one of the stops on the Carson and Colorado Railroad.

William Sharon, Hume Yerington and Darius Mills formed the Carson and Colorado Company in 1880. A narrow gauge railroad, it would start at Mound House, Nevada, near Carson City, and run via the Owens Valley to the Colorado River, thus giving it the name "Carson and Colorado." However, the building of the railroad stopped at Keeler, many miles short of the Colorado River.

Upon receiving word that the railroad would run east of the Owens River, people began arriving in the area. A surveyor laid out a town site. Before long it became a small town with well planned streets, houses, stores and, yes, outhouses. By the time crews finished laying the tracks and the train rolled in, the depot, agent's house, section boss' house, water tank and turntable were ready.

It took three years to lay the track from Mound House to Station and another six months to finish laying the rails to Keeler.

Being the first station built on the line from Mound House to Keeler, the company gave the little town the name "Station." After the completion of twenty-two other stations, the town was renamed "Laws," after R. J. Laws, an Assistant Superintendent who became Superintendent when the Southern Pacific bought the line in 1900.

As time went on the townspeople built more houses and businesses and Laws became a thriving town. It consisted of at least two stores, a post office, a pool hall, an eating house and hotel, pool room and dance hall, a barber shop and blacksmith shop, as well as other businesses.

The railroad became an invaluable means of transportation for people and property. To the north, everything and everyone came into or went out of the valley by train. To and from the south, people and merchandise traveled by wagon and stagecoach to Lone Pine or Keeler and by train the rest of the way. In 1908 the Southern Pacific built a standard gauge rail line from Mojave to Owenyo, next to Keeler. Everyone prospered from this, especially farmers, businessmen, mine owners and the power company. Roads, in those days, were no more than rough, dirt trails making road travel slow and quite uncomfortable.

Farmers shipped their products including livestock, poultry, hay, wool and honey to markets in Nevada and sold them to the boom mining camps. This produce also found its way to larger markets in the San Francisco bay area---all shipped from Laws via the Narrow Gauge.

Laws and the Carson and Colorado railroad played an important role in the development of the Bishop Creek/Cardinal Mine since the railroad operated during the mine's entire existence. In the early part of the twentieth century, shipping on the narrow gauge was the best means of transportation for the region, far superior to hauling by team and wagon. Essentially all of the equipment, large and small, installed at the mine came in on the railroad, from small electric motors to a six ton tube mill. The train brought in everything used, from buckets to barrels of chemicals; from hand tools to huge spools of cable; from food to tons of coal. And the mining companies shipped their products out by rail, as well.

The power company with its plants along Bishop Creek also relied on the railroad to bring in equipment and supplies.

Most of the miners and power company workers brought their families in on the train, complete with household goods, furniture and even poultry and livestock. Mr. and Mrs. Gleason Coen of Bishop tell a story about the arrival to the area of Florence Kennedy (now deceased). She and her sister, both young girls at the time, and their mother, came in on the Slim Princess from Garden Grove, arriving on Christmas eve' in 1912. They brought everything they owned with them, all their personal belongings, their furniture, chickens, cows and a horse. They came to the area to live on a 40 acre farm located in the vicinity of Barlow Lane. Their father met them at the station and escorted them home in a buggy with a fringe on top. Their friends had warned them that the Indians in the area would "scalp them." The ride home was quite scary. The next morning when they awoke, they were petrified to see an Indian lady looking in the window at them. They thought, "Just one night here and we're gone!" They soon found that the Indians in the area were very friendly and it was not uncommon for them to look in a window, now and then, out of curiosity.

In 1905, the company updated the tracks which went from Mound House to Mina, Nevada, to standard gauge and moved the narrow gauge shops to Mina. In 1943, they stopped service from Mina to Laws and removed the tracks. Then, on April 30, 1960, the last train made its run between Laws and Keeler. Southern Pacific gave the following reasons for abandoning service: "declining and unpredictable use of line, . . . expensive and time consuming transfer of shipments between narrow gauge (small sized cars) and standard gauge cars" and "action unavoidable though regrettable from a sentimental point of view." The Laws-Keeler branch of the Southern Pacific was the last operating narrow gauge public carrier west of the Rocky Mountains.

On this date, too, the Southern Pacific Railway Co. formally transferred locomotive No. 9 (a ten wheel Baldwin built in 1909), a string of cars, the Laws Station Building and surrounding railroad installations, jointly, to the City of Bishop and the County of Inyo in the form of a "Gift Deed." The Slim Princess as a part of railroad history ended. It became a legend.

Southern Pacific donated approximately eleven acres of land to Inyo County in July of 1964. In January of 1965, the Bishop Museum and Historical Society negotiated an agreement with Inyo County and the City of Bishop to take over the Laws site as Headquarters with permission to operate a museum.

The Laws Railroad Museum opened its doors to the public on April 1, 1966, exactly 83 years after the first train arrived at Laws from the north. The museum is located approximately five miles north east of Bishop just off Highway 6, on Silver Canyon Road.

After the Cardinal Mine closed in 1938, many items, both industrial and personal, remained at the site. The property stood vacant until the late 1940s; by then, many of the items had been disposed of in various ways. Mr. and Mrs. Wells Hall obtained the property in 1951 and operated it for fifteen years. When they sold to the Neschers, the Halls decided to preserve some of the artifacts left at the site by giving them to the Laws Railroad Museum, which they did on May 8, 1966.

The following is a list of the items along with their present location:

S. Nakashima Photo.

Footed, fluted, Carnival glass bowl, grape leaf and cluster design, gold iridescent and dark blue color, formerly owned by the Lovering family (originally from Leeds, South Dakota), stands on the dining room table in the agent's house.

Hard tire trailer, old hand cultivator, large wood-

Large wooden wheel.   SN Photo.

en wheel and small wooden wheel (broken), are all located across from the agent's house.

Forty-six various bottles are now scattered throughout the bottle house.

A Davis sewing machine, treadle type with attachments, found in one of the vacant miner's houses, sits in a bedroom in the Shaw House.

Other items, now being stored at the museum are: Ball tongs, toboggan, old hand truck, two cabinet maker's wooden planes, stove (cabin heater from mine area), tatting shuttle and a Bodie Miners Index, dated Dec. 4, 1897.

The museum hopes to eventually take these items out of storage and display them to the public.

REFERENCES AND NOTES

Laws Railroad Museum.

Bob Dinsmore and Alice Boothe of the Laws Railroad Museum.

Interviews with Barbara Cluff and Gleason Coen.

Hard tire trailer once used at the mine.   SN Photo.

Small wooden pulley wheel probably
used on one of the head frames.

SN Photo.

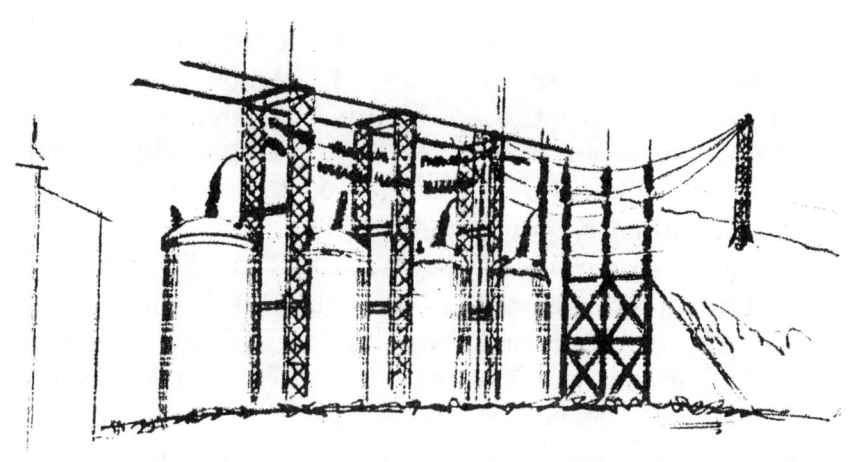

CHAPTER
VII

THE POWER COMPANIES

The power companies that served the Bishop Creek/Cardinal Gold Mine and the surrounding area have a long and interesting history since their inception in 1902. Although the mine did not receive power from the companies until 1932, they played a substantial enough part in the history of the mine that a history of the power companies should be included as well.

The Bishop Light and Power Company organized the county's first electric enterprise in 1902 to supply the needs of the local people. The Nevada-California Power Company bought them out in May 1909 for approximately $34,000.

In 1904, a couple of fellows, Loren Curtis, a hydraulic engineer and Charles M. Hobbs, came from Denver (by way of the gold mines in Tonopah) to the Bishop region in search of gold. They discovered Bishop Creek instead. They realized that harnessing the water coming down Bishop Creek would be more profitable than mining. Backed by Denver financiers, they built a hydroelectric power plant on Bishop Creek to supply the mines of Tonopah and Goldfield, Nevada. They organized the Nevada Power, Mining & Milling Company on December 31, 1904, reorganizing in 1906, under the new name, Nevada-California Power Co.

Actual construction work began on the first power plant on January 1, 1905, with the completion of Plant 4 within a few months. From there, they constructed a 113-mile transmission line, crossing the White Mountains at an elevation of 10,500 feet, to Tonopah and Goldfield. At that time it was the longest transmission line in the world. This was a great boon to both the power company and the mining companies. Eventually, the Wilshire Bishop Creek Gold Company would profit as well.

The narrow gauge railroad brought train after train load of ponderous generators and other machinery to Laws for construction of the plants and transmission lines. Freighters laboriously hauled these heavy loads up to the plant site using long strings of mules. Forty-two head plus six pushing behind, were put in service for the heaviest loads. One can see a set of big wooden wheels from one of those wagons, at Plant 4. Pack trains and buckboard wagons carried material along an ever-lengthening road following the construction of the power lines.

R. J. Schober and George C. Kinney contracted with the power company to transport equipment and material from the Laws Railroad Station up to the power plants. To haul the tremendous loads they used a total of 60 horses and 20 specially built wagons. One of their wagons, locally called "a Goliath among vehicles," weighed several tons. Schober and Kinney charged the power company approximately $17.00 a ton to haul the loads.

Hauling these heavy loads certainly caused the freighters their share of problems. In 1913, while hauling a transformer weighing close to 48 tons, they hit a soft spot in the road between Laws and Bishop, dropping the transformer from the wagon. A day or so later, while crossing a bridge over Bishop Creek, one of the wagon wheels broke through the bridge and again dropped the transformer from the wagon, this time into the creek.

The Nevada Power Company saw not only the importance of the water power of Bishop Creek but the need to conserve the spring runoff, to be used later. The first dam built was at Intake II. Then in 1906-07, the company built a dam creating a lake they officially called Intake I but later renamed Lake Sabrina, for the Superintendent's wife, Sabrina Hobbs. Subsequently, the company built dams at North Lake and South Lake (previously called Hillside Reservoir). Over the next few years, the company completed Plants 2, 3, 5 and 6. They cleared an area for a Plant 1, however, that plant never materialized.

Since Bishop Creek falls 5,500 feet in fourteen miles, it enables the power plants in tandem to use the same water five times to generate power. When it reaches the bottom, it is as pure as it was when it came out of the back country. A very efficient system, indeed.

The power company received a crippling and expensive blow on June 24,1909. Due to the heavy flow of surplus water from Lake Sabrina, excess pressure caused the Intake II dam to break. This put the entire power system out of commission, throwing Tonopah, Goldfield, Rhyolite and other Nevada towns, as well as the towns of Bishop and Laws, into total darkness. The flood completely swamped the intake to the water system, putting the whole town of Bishop without water.

At Plant 4, the first warning was the roar of the water and in a few seconds, Bishop Creek came up to the buildings, the water flowing through the machine shop and threatening to swamp the dynamo house. All operation of the plant ceased immediately. Farther down the canyon, the torrent washed out the road in several places. It killed six horses belonging to Charles Phelps, and injured several others. The water cut channels through several farms and through the wheat fields of C. E. Johnson, washing away the top soil. John Dugan, William McLaren, N. J. Cooley, Ike Squires and the Kilpatrick estate also received damage from the raging water.

The Power Company eventually rebuilt the Intake II dam of concrete, to higher construction standards, and it remains reliable to this date.

In those days, every intake and every lake had a caretaker. The caretaker of Intake II and Plant 2 lived in a cabin located near the dam. That cabin was eventually destroyed by an avalanche in 1969.

By 1910, near exhaustion of the big mines forced the power company to seek a new marketplace for its power. In 1912, they formed a subsidiary, the Southern Sierras Power Company. This new company built a 238 mile power line across the Eastern Mojave Desert and over Cajon Pass to San Bernardino and Riverside Counties. They obtained franchises to provide power to communities such as Rialto, Corona, Hemet, and Elsinore. They also served small communities in the desolate desert areas such as Barstow, Victorville,

Randsburg and Inyokern.

From 1909 until 1932, the Bishop Creek Mining Company generated its own power using the stream coming down the mountainside from North Lake. The Southern Sierras Power Company wanted the right to use that water, so they made a trade with the mining company. The power company ran a power line from Intake II (a line was already in place from Plant 2 to Intake II) and furnished power to the mine at a very favorable rate, for the use of the water coming out of North Lake. The first 300 horsepower was free; the charge for the next 1,200 horsepower was $3 per horsepower month. All power over 1,500 horsepower was charged at the regular rates. A crew accomplished the task of laying the line and hooking up the power in just one day.

One of the prominent names in the history of the power company was Ernest Irl "Ernie" Bulpitt. Born in 1895, his family lived on a farm called Abelor Ranch, now the location of the Millpond recreation area. He started working for the power company in 1920 with a construction crew, building the Gem Lake Dam. In 1925, he was appointed Chief Hydrographer for the power company. He retired in 1962 as the manager of California Electric Company, Northern Division.

Aside from his outstanding career, Bulpitt was a dedicated family man as well as a leader in the community, excelling in the American Legion, Elks and Masons. He leased property on Bishop Creek in the west part of Bishop, and maintained the "Bulpitt Park" for use by the towns people, for many years. The Elks now manage the park, renaming it "Elks Park."

Another distinguished gentleman who worked with the company for many years is Mr. Gleason Coen, now living in Bishop with his wife, Irene. Mr. Coen started working for Nevada-California Power Company in 1929 as a transformer coil winder. During his years of employment, Coen worked in many capacities and accomplished numerous positive advances for the company. For example, he initiated the automation of valves at the intakes, eliminating the need for a caretaker at each site. The area covered by crews in his charge ranged from Inyokern to Bridgeport.

He spent the last three years with the company working at Hoover Dam as the Resident Engineer. He said it was a bit hard to get used to having "five million yards of concrete for an office." He retired in 1967 after working for the company for 38 years.

The power company grew and expanded, and changed names several times. Its long, colorful history will not be included here as it has already been covered in other books.

The following lists the succession of power companies and their dates of operation.

1902 - 1909   Bishop Light and Power Co.
1904 - 1906   Nevada Power, Mining and Milling Co.
1906 - 1936   Nevada - California Power Co.
1912 - 1936   Southern Sierras Power Co. (A
                       subsidiary of NE-CA Power Co.)
1936 - 1941   Nevada - California Electric Corp.
1941 - 1963   California Electric Power Co.
1963 - present   Southern California Edison Co.
                       In 1969, Sierra Pacific Power Co.
                       purchased the Nevada properties.

Life at the power company sites very closely resembled that of the Cardinal Village. Located in remote, primitive areas, both developed close knit communities.

Each power plant maintained its own little neighborhood. Families lived year round in homes built on the sites. Plants 2 and 3 contained several houses while Plant 4 had more than twenty. An elementary school was also located at Plant 4.

There were a few rules, early on. Because of their isolation, families with children were never allowed to live at Plant 2, nor at Plant 3 until 1945. They had no school and no ready access to doctors. Also, the power company required the people who lived at those two plants to lay in a three months supply of groceries and a 60 day supply of stove oil before the beginning of winter. Because of the primitive road conditions in winter, no one knew when they would be completely cut off from the rest of the world.

Shortly after he arrived in Bishop from Cambria, at the age of 15, George Williams (still living in Bishop) worked at the Safeway Store in town. One of his jobs was to fill the orders sent down by the folks at Plants 2 and 3. He remembers well delivering the supplies up the canyon to their homes. He also recalls a story told by his father, Elzie Williams, a shift boss at one of the power plants. The company asked Elzie to take some equipment to one of the power plants. There was no snow removal at the time. Williams actually put snow shoes on the horses to navigate over the deep drifts.

Gleason Coen lived at Plant 2 when he started working for the company. He recalls a switchboard at the site, installed by the telephone company. An operator there relayed the calls to the Bishop Creek Mine and the Schober Pack Stations. Coen remembers, "The mine even received calls from as far away as Europe."

Harvey and Louise Dougherty could be considered a typical "power plant family;" they lived "up the canyon" for many years. Harvey Dougherty (now deceased) worked for the power company for 32 years.

Louise Dougherty of Bishop has wonderful memories of their life on the creek. They lived for many years at their first home at Plant 3. Because of their isolation and cabin fever, the Doughertys, along with other neighbors and the help of Ernie Bulpitt, started a square dance group. They would walk down to Plant 4, a distance of two and a half miles, dance all evening, then walk back to Plant 3, arriving home about 2 A.M. "Going home was much the harder direction!" Louise recalls. At same time, they also delivered mail to the Plant 3 residents.

Some of the residents raised gardens. Deer, who were plentiful and quite bold, proved a constant problem, eating anything they planted. One morning Harvey Dougherty awoke to find a big buck looking in the bedroom window. He reached out and grabbed it by the antler; the frightened deer bounded off to safety.

Today, the Dougherty's son, Dean, works for the power company. He lives at Plant 6 with his family in a house built in 1868, previously known as the "West Bishop Mill House." Dean grew up at Plants 3 and 4, remembering the area as "the ideal place for a boy to grow up."

The Doughertys later moved to Plant 4. In winter the boys walked upstream to Plant 3, then came down the two and a half miles on their sleds---in five minutes! In summer they followed the same route, only body surfing the stream back to their home. They had another favorite activity in the summer. The young entrepreneurs set up a lemonade stand on the highway at the location where upcoming cars had to stop and let their radiators cool. They sold fresh, home-made lemonade for 10 cents a glass, making up to $5.30 in one day. They also sold chocolate chip cookies. (Louise remembers hand squeezing lots of lemons and baking lots of cookies!) And the folks coming up the old road were happy to buy refreshments at that point.

A wonderful club house was located at Plant 4, the showcase of the community. Many people ate their meals there, prepared by the cooks, Mr. and Mrs. Godlove. The club house was the social center for all the people living on the creek. Later, the power company demolished the club house, all the homes at Plants 2 and 3 and some at Plants 4 and 5. It was a very sad time. Louise recalls, "Almost every one cried."

Many more "typical" families lived on Bishop Creek in the early days. There are numerous wonderful stories yet untold. Company workers still live at Plants 4, 5 and 6 and it remains a great place to live and bring up children. Much has changed, however; automobiles and better roads make life a lot easier.

But there are still many people around who remember the "good old days!"

Southern California Edison Photo.

A long string of mules hauling heavy generator parts from Laws to the Bishop Creek Power Plants. Similar teams were used to haul heavy equipment to the Bishop Creek Mine. It is almost impossible to imagine this contingent negotiating the curves and steep grades up the mountain to their destination.

Plant 4 as it appeared in 1923.   Southern California Edison Photo.

REFERENCES AND NOTES

Owens Valley Herald: May 7, 1909; June 25, 1909.

The Southern California Edison Company.

U. S. Department of Interior "Information Circular" dated May 1938, "Milling Methods and Costs of the Cardinal Gold Mining Co." written by Walter B. Lenhart.

Interviews with Juanita and Rick Apted, Gleason Coen, Louise and Dean Dougherty, Mr. and Mrs. Gibb Kieser, Yan Kinney and George Williams.

Horse's snow shoe belonging to George Williams of Bishop.

CHAPTER
VIII

HENRY GAYLORD WILSHIRE

Henry Gaylord Wilshire was born to George Wilshire (a wealthy businessman) and Clara Clemons Wilshire in Cincinnati, Ohio, on June 7, 1861. After attending Harvard University, Wilshire became manager of his father's rolling mill in Cincinnati in 1882.

An ambitious, energetic and progressive young man, Wilshire was always looking for a better position in life. After two years at his father's mill, he moved to San Francisco to work in a lock, scale and safe business owned by his brother, William.

In 1886, after only two years there, Gaylord and his brother moved to Los Angeles and, with their father's instructions and money, began to speculate in the Southern California land boom. Over the next couple of years, they invested in real estate in the cities of Long Beach, Los Angeles, Pasadena, and Santa Monica and in Orange County.

Unlike many other local developers, Griffith, Doheney and Mulholland, Wilshire was a nonconformist entrepreneur. He developed an interest in the socialistic point of view and joined the socialist party in 1887. It is important to note that although he was a socialist, his views differed considerably from the Marxist brand of socialism which later emerged in Russia. Wilshire adopted the Fabian socialist point of view which rejected Marxism, promoted evolutionary socialism and denied the need for violent class struggle.

He took advantage of his blue-blood birth to launch attacks on aristocrats who controlled the country's economy; for this he earned the title, "Socialist Millionaire."

Wilshire became close friends with authors Jack London, George Bernard Shaw, H. G. Wells, and Upton Sinclair, the socialist rabble-rouser who managed to get himself arrested for reading the Constitution to his listeners in a public park, without a permit.

Gaylord Wilshire was an independent and visionary man who went his own way in the world. When land speculation began to falter in 1888, he experimented with other investments, among them an ostrich farm in Anaheim. William Wilshire returned to San Francisco, and Gaylord settled down to try his hand at ranching in Orange County. He grew walnuts and citrus fruits in an area now known as Fullerton, a town for which he is partially credited for founding. He not only introduced grapefruit as a crop into Orange County, but helped to transform his seaside play land into the city of Long Beach. Later he became director of a Fullerton bank, quite in opposition to his Socialistic beliefs.

In 1889, along with William C. Owen, Wilshire

founded the "Weekly Nationalist", a socialist paper in Los Angeles. By 1890, he was very involved in politics and the socialist party and became the first socialist to run for a seat in the United States Congress. Although he did not win, he did receive a respectable number of votes in California's Sixth Congressional District.

More than his upper crust position or Harvard education, it was the handsome Wilshire's unpredictable antics and wit that gained support for his platform. Known as a political P.T. Barnum, he once ran for public office challenging his opponent to a $10,000 debate and gambling that the audience would side with him. His opponent declined but Wilshire gained considerable media attention.

Wilshire's split social status tended to amuse rather than threaten the Hearst-and-Rockefeller set. Although he preferred the company of the literary liberals, he enjoyed bedeviling the elite and reporting their activities back to the public.

Attending dinner one evening at the home of Lady Warwick, he invited her chimney sweep whom he'd met outside to join him. When the Warwicks informed him that his guest was improperly attired, Wilshire ate with the sweep in the kitchen, swapping stories over bottles of French wine while the others gossiped from behind the dining room door.

In early 1890, Wilshire lost his father but received a sizable inheritance from his estate.

During the latter part of that year, rumors were circulating that Wilshire and Hanna Owen (wife of Wilshire's partner, William) were "carrying on." The San Francisco newspaper, the Los Angeles Times, and Wilshire's home town paper, Cincinnati's "Commercial Gazette," carried the story that intimacy between Wilshire and Mrs. Owen had forced a divorce between she and Mr. Owen. Wilshire published an article in the Gazette on November 27, strongly denying the accusation, saying "the article is palpably ridiculous" and "the whole dispatch is but a tissue of falsehoods."

However, Gaylord and Hanna had become legally married on November 14. Perhaps the scandal contributed to the short life of this marriage for they were divorced not long after.

In 1891, "Comrade Wilshire" set out on a trip to London to meet the Fabian Socialistic idols. Stopping off in New York, his Nationalist friends encouraged him to become the Socialist candidate for state Attorney General. Although he lost the election, he managed to gain 15,000 votes for the Socialists. He then took up residence in London and became a renowned lecturer.

In 1893, Wilshire got the nomination as the Social Democratic Federation candidate for Parliament. For unknown reasons, he returned to the United States before the election took place.

Upon his return to Los Angeles in 1895, he developed the "Wilshire Tract." Spotting some vacant property extending west from down town Los Angeles, he put a wide street he called Wilshire Boulevard down the middle of it. He thus initiated the swank westward extension of the city that later went on to include the Miracle Mile, continued on to Beverly Hills, and eventually to the ocean.

After a previous, unsuccessful attempt at magazine publishing, Wilshire created a new socialist paper known as "The Challenge." In 1900 he moved it to New York City. Because of an attempt to keep radical publishers out of the city, postal authorities would not give him second class mailing privileges. This did not discourage Wilshire, he moved it to Canada and renamed the magazine, "Wilshire's Magazine."

On May 17, 1901, the Los Angeles Times ran an article with the headline "H. Gaylord Pulled for Blowing off in Park." It seems Wilshire had called the police station and asked them to arrest him for speaking in Central Park without a permit, even suggesting a date and time. In a note to them he said, "I would like to be arrested at, say, 4:30 o'clock, Thursday afternoon, if convenient to you."

His motive was two-fold. He delighted in publicity, but he also wanted a sensational article to promote his magazine. In the same note to the police, he added, "It is not only a matter of sentiment with me, but it is also a matter of business. I am publishing a weekly paper which does considerable blowing about the menace of plutocracy. A paper needs an ad to obtain a good circulation and any stick is good enough to beat a dog, you know." He further suggested they send the "ugliest and most brutal officer on the force" in a patrol wagon in "apple-pie order" as he intended sending pictures of the scene throughout the east where his paper was circulated.

Both Wilshire and the police kept the engagement. At the appointed hour, Wilshire made a few choice remarks to an apathetic knot of wind-jammers and sleepy loafers holding down the benches in Central Park. "Commodore" Hill, the big park officer had arrived to take Wilshire to the station---in a car! Wilshire was crushed. He had requested the patrol wagon. His impassioned pleading finally prevailed; the officer gave in and sent for the wagon. Wilshire fairly beamed with joy as he rode off. At the station, he enthusiastically paid the $50 bail and asked what court he would be tried in.

Wilshire's was a lavish magazine and a terrible drain on his finances. In order to support his political interests, he needed another investment. This led him to invest in the Wilshire mines, the Bishop Creek Gold Mine near Bishop, California, and the Tassawini and Aremu Gold mines located in British Guiana. Along with several other men, he reorganized the Bishop Creek Gold Company in New York City in 1906, and became the Secretary/Treasurer of the company, offering his personal stock in the mine for sale.

He advertised the Bishop Creek Gold Company property in the September 1906 issue of Wilshire's Magazine as the "World's Greatest Gold Mine." In one column of the advertisement, under the heading, "Special to Wilshire's Subscribers," he wrote:

". . . I have been on the lookout for a good gold mining proposition and now I think that I have at last found one in the Bishop Creek Mine, of Inyo County, California," and "I expect to use my share in the gold from this wonderful mine to teach the gospel of Socialism. Nothing like money to fight money."

One of the driving forces in Wilshire's involvement with the mine was his desire to possess a mine greater than the Homestake Gold Mine in Lead, South Dakota, owned by his friend, William Randolph Hearst. Unfortunately, this never materialized.

Wilshire's personal life took on a new dimension when, in 1904 he married Mary Reynolds, a lay-psycho-analyst. She received her training in psychology under the famous Swiss psychologist and professor, Carl Jung. The Wilshire's had a son, Logan, born in 1906, their only child.

By the spring of 1907, Wilshire envisioned a type of socialist utopian community centered at the mine with perhaps 300 to 400 socialists working by that summer. However, his dreams for the camp never materialized. An article in the Inyo Register dated September 18, 1908, notes that "at no time since April 1907, has there been less than ten men employed upon the property, and the force has reached as high as 50 men."

The same article mentions that some of the men had brought their families to live in cabins on the property. In fact, Gaylord Wilshire and his family spent the summer at the camp. They used the property intermittently as a vacation spot at which to relax and entertain friends. The Wilshires and the Jack Londons sometimes used a cabin on the mine property as a hide-away where they could do their writing.

By 1908, Wilshire had become president and owner of the Wilshire/Bishop Creek Gold Company.

The mine development work and the purchase of mine and mill equipment was costly. By 1910, the Post Office Department began an investigation of claims by stockholders (many of whom were Socialists) that fraud was connected with the sale of Bishop Creek Mine stock. Wilshire moved his family to London to escape the investigation. In 1911, he received a letter from Postmaster J. W. Clark of Bishop, stating his faith in the mining venture and dropping the fraud case.

Finally in early 1914, at the outbreak of World War I, Wilshire returned to Los Angeles. In November of that year, Wilshire moved his wife, Mary, and their eight year old son, Logan, to Bishop from England. They leased the Eugene Smith house and spent the winter in Bishop.

By 1915, Wilshire realized that his personal fortune was dwindling. He reorganized the Bishop Creek Mine under the name Consolidated Wilshire Mining Company. However, this did not pay off and the mine was operational only intermittently over the next several years.

Undefeated, he attempted to regain his fortune by trying his hand at various business ventures over the next several years. His unsuccessful enterprises included real estate speculation, health foods, and a health spa. No longer financially able to operate the mine after 1922, Wilshire leased the property. Finally, Mary became the sole support of her family. This was a terrible blow to the pride of the arrogant, H. Gaylord Wilshire.

During the next few years he searched in vain for another business venture that could replace his lost fortunes.

Although Wilshire had no formal training in science, it always held a fascination for him. Because of this interest, he eventually invented the "Ionaco", a cure-all which came to be known as the "magic horse collar." It consisted of a coil of wire some two feet in diameter, enclosed in a leather-like cover, which was to be put over one shoulder or around the body at chest or abdomen, depending on where the illness was centered, and plugged into a light socket.

A friend of the family, Dr. David Winkler, now living in Santa Barbara, recalls hearing Mr. Wilshire expounding its virtues to the headmaster of a boarding school he was attending. Wilshire told them about the iron molecules in the blood cells, which would respond to the current and line up with their magnetic north poles all pointed one way, or perhaps flipping back and forth with the alternating current. This was a garble of pseudo science that Gaylord Wilshire no doubt believed wholly, making him a good salesman. And sure enough, the school became another owner of the magic horse collar! Dr. Winkler remembers big billboards advertising it, showing a man seated with this thing draped around him and the words "Wilshire's Ionaco" in big letters on the billboard.

Wilshire arranged for the belts to be manufactured by Westinghouse, and by 1926, sales boomed in his distributing offices throughout the west. These profits were short lived, however, for in 1927 he was investigated for fraudulent claims. His attorney stated that "Wilshire never intended to mislead the public concerning the therapeutic effects of the belt and that the inventor honestly believed that he was helping mankind."

Legal claims against the company ended abruptly when, on September 27, 1927, Wilshire died of heart failure in New York City.

Enterprising and adventurous Gaylord Wilshire died never to know that his dream of buried wealth in the mountains west of Bishop eventually would be realized. The Cardinal Gold Mining Company operating on the old Wilshire/Bishop Creek Gold Mining property became, in 1937, one of the leading producers of gold in California.

Los Angeles' prestigious Wilshire Boulevard bears no stars on its sidewalk, yet its founder, Henry Gaylord Wilshire, was a celebrity in his own right, a rich rebel with a cause who left behind a colorful legend. And his development of wide, automotive-friendly boulevards along with his unbridled spirit still represent Los Angeles today.

*　*　*　*　*　*　*　*

Gaylord Wilshire's wife, Mary, lived for some thirty years after his death. A close friend of hers, Dr. David Winkler, recalls Mary, her unusual outlook on life and her wonderful personality. The following is a part of his description of her: "She was 'middle aged' all the time I knew her, all the thirty years, by which I mean she was ageless, old enough to be very wise and above entanglements but without a trace of aging, or loss of the sharpness, awareness and sensitivity of her mind. She said she did not know how old she was and did not care."

Mary was very devoted to her son, Logan; to her he could do no wrong. Logan was a lean, intense person and very self-centered; he had none of Mary's sensitivity to people and understanding of them. And he lived in a fantasy world, built largely on Mary's image of him as an unusually brilliant young man.

For quite some time he was a perpetual student, writing a book on philosophy or so Mary said, and on the verge of being recognized for the depth and wisdom of his work. As far as David Winkler knew, Logan never obtained his PhD nor finished his book. Eventually he had to earn his own living, became a stock broker, and then married a school teacher. The date of his death is not known; perhaps his widow is the only living member of the family.

Many years after David Winkler had last seen Mary, he called on her and found her lying abed because she lacked the strength to sit up. She allowed the restrictions of old age gradually to close in on her, because she had no choice. Lying quietly there she said, "At last I have time to think."

Knowing that Mary had always been a thinker, Winkler interpreted her remark in this way, "She was I believe alluding to the fact that she could now turn off the rest of the world as she turned off her television. There was no more reading and no more letter writing to be done. She could retreat now into the lovely, rich garden of her memories."

REFERENCES AND NOTES

FEDCO Reporter, April, 1992, pg. 12. The story, "The Socialist Millionaire of Los Angeles" written by Judith Blocker Uthus, a free-lance writer from Santa Monica.

Roberta Nichols' "The Many Lives of H. Gaylord Wilshire," a Los Cerritos Docents Publication, Sep. 1977, pp. 8-13;   Dec. 1977, pp. 5-12.

Inyo Register: Apr. 4, 1907; Sep. 18, 1908; June 23, 1910; Jan. 12, 1911; May 28, 1914; Nov. 6, 1914; Nov. 14, 1914;   Apr. 30, 1915.

Los Angeles Times: Dec. 5, 1890; May 17, 1901.

Wilshire's Magazine, September 1906.

Interviews with Barbara Cluff and David Winkler.

CHAPTER
IX

THE CARDINAL VILLAGE TODAY

From April through October, visitors to the Cardinal Village Resort find a bustling, happy atmosphere. Fishermen gather in the store to share stories about "the big one that got away." Hal and Barbara Cluff and their friendly staff greet everyone who enters with a smile and a cheery "Hello." The homey, family atmosphere about the place recalls the spirit of the families of the old mining days. Much quieter in the winter, the Cluffs close the store and restaurant but rent the cabins to the snow lovers who visit the area.

When the mine closed in September, 1938, workers moved on to other areas to begin new lives and the Cardinal Village closed its doors. It stood vacant from 1938 to the late 1940s when Peter McLaurin purchased the complex and turned it into a fisherman's resort. Wells and Bernice Hall bought the property in 1951 and operated it for fifteen years. They sold it in 1966 to the Neschers who in turn sold it in 1968 to the Strattons.

Larry and Nadine Stratton will never forget September 26, 1982, when the North Lake Dam broke, sending a torrent of water down to engulf the Cardinal Village Resort. Nadine reported, "We're like an island, completely surrounded by water. We're sitting in the lodge with blankets and a fireplace; just sitting here, lighting candles and trying to keep warm." After several weeks of hard labor and a lot of money, the Strattons managed to put the Lodge back into operating condition.

After seventeen years of operation, Larry and Nadine Stratton sold the resort in 1985 to Hal and Barbara Cluff, the present owners.

A store, a post office, a schoolhouse, a meat house, the paymasters quarters, and about 100 cabins remained at the close of the mining operation in 1938. Raymond Milovich of Bishop recalls that "Kirk" Otey moved twenty-one of these buildings down the old, one way road to his Otey Village just west of Bishop. All those homes are gone now; all that remains today is a short street called Otey Road, connecting Red Hill Road and Highway 168. The Otey Store was moved up the steep, winding road to Aspendell. It is now the home of Ken and Avis Stroman.

Many buildings were moved or torn down; no record was kept as to where they went or what happened to them.

Thirteen buildings remain in the Cardinal Village today. Cabins *Topsy Turvy*, *Loch Leven*, and *Emerald*,

Loch Leven cabin, once a family home. Cluff Photo.

were built in 1906 as family residences. Cabins *Moonlight, Midnight,* and *Lamarch,* also built in 1906, were bunkhouses. One cabin remaining, *Baboon,* is actually two one-room cabins put together; it is not known when this was done, however, it was used as a bunkhouse for the miners.

The old stable was built in 1906. In 1946, the Cardinal Resort owners made it into a store and cafe. Later, they completely refurbished the building and made it into a two-story cabin, now called *Golden Trout.*

The cabin *Blue Lake* was originally built in 1906 as the cookhouse. It burned to the ground in the early 1930s and was rebuilt using metal siding. It was then used as a bunkhouse.

The *Cardinal Lodge* building (restaurant, store and bait and tackle shop), originally a square building,

The Lodge as it appeared in 1946 or 1947   Stratton Photo

was also built in 1906 and used as the Paymaster's Lodge. When the cookhouse burned, the Cardinal Mining Company built an addition onto the paymaster's lodge for the new cookhouse. Later, they added three more additions, making it now quite a complex floor plan.

The meat house, built in 1895, is the oldest building at the Cardinal Village.   SN Photo.

The oldest building remaining but no longer in use is the *Meat House,* built in 1895. It still stands between two streams with a small board bridge giving access to the building, just as it was one hundred years ago.

Still in use, the *transformer building* contains the electrical equipment for the compound.

In 1970-71 the Cardinal Resort owners built a

duplex, *Thunder and Lightning,* as a rental cabin.

All of the rental cabins at the Cardinal Resort have names taken from lakes in the Sabrina Basin. John and Art Schober named these lakes during the 1930s when they were hired by the Department of Fish and Game to stock them with fish.

The former Post Office/Commissary is today,   SN Photo.
the residence of Mr. & Mrs. G. G. Kieser.

In 1946, the parents of Mrs. G. G. Kieser bought the post office/commissary building, located just outside the village property, from the General Commissary Company. The Kiesers converted it to a family dwelling, moving all the post office equipment and supplies to the post office in Bishop. It is believed this was passed on to the Laws Railroad Museum. During its use in the mining days, the company sectioned off one corner of the store for a card room where miners gathered to play their favorite game, Pangini.

The original builders painted all these buildings a

rust-brown with white trim around the doors and windows with the exception of the post office/commissary which was painted dark green. They still look the same today as they did during the old mining days. The modern era building, *Thunder and Lightning,* displays the same exterior features as the older buildings.

The Old Chevron gas pump stands in front of the Lodge.

Two other buildings of consequence are no longer located at the village. The school house, also used as the church and ironically named after Drunken Sailor Lake, remained in place for many years. It was located on Forest Service land just outside the Resort property. Although the owners of the Cardinal put up a good fight, the Forest Service, in 1987, insisted it must be torn down and disposed of, thus losing a valuable and interesting landmark.

In 1986, the Schobers purchased Blue Heaven cabin, built in the Cardinal era, and moved it to their Pack Station at North Lake where it is still used as a bunk house for the packers.

John and Art Schober dug the Cardinal Pond in 1934, using only a team of horses, a slip scraper, and a plow. It is located just across the little meadow from the front of the Lodge. It may have been created as an irrigation pond for the camp garden. Today the Depart-

Emerald cabin, once a family residence.   SN Photo.

ment of Fish and Game keeps it stocked with trout. During the summer months, young and old alike find it a most popular fishing spot.

A log house, constructed sometime before 1928, once stood on a ridge to the west-southwest of the lodge building. Some sources indicate it was built by Gaylord Wilshire as a residence to be used by his family when they visited the area. It acquired the name "Supervisor's House," indicating it may have housed the mine supervisor at some time.

For several years, beginning in about 1928, it was occupied by a lady named Ruth Sherman. It is not known how many years she lived there or what her association was with the mine. Mary Wilshire, wife of the late Henry Gaylord Wilshire, visited her frequently. Mary, a lay-psychoanalyst, saw some of her clients at the supervisor's house.

Sometime in the late 1930s, the house was dismantled and reconstructed at a site near the Camp

Golden Trout was once the stable, then store and cafe and now, a large cabin.

SN Photo.

Sabrina area. The movers numbered each log and piece of the building and replaced them in their original position. Only the chimney could not be moved. It still stands like a sentinel and can be seen from the road leading up to Lake Sabrina. Other remains in the area are the foundation, the fireplace at the base of the chimney, and a line of rocks surrounding the yard.

In summertime, fishermen and hikers rent cabins at the Cardinal Village Resort. In wintertime, cross-country skiers and snow lovers in general rent the cabins. The restaurant and store, with its bait and tackle shop, remain open only during fishing season, from the last weekend in April to the last weekend in October.

During the summer months, the Cluffs offer a special dinner every Saturday evening, by reservation only. Barbara makes salad, baked potatoes and dessert inside the restaurant; Hal barbecues steak and chicken on his outdoor barbecue. One can eat either indoors or on the picnic tables outside. The feeling is that of one big happy family. Hal calls it, "Dinner at the Cluffs."

The Cluffs operate the Cardinal Village Resort with the assistance of several young people involved in YWAM (Youth With a Mission). Hal and Barbara, leaders in this missionary program, have on several occasions, sent their young missionaries to Croatia. Hal and Barbara too, have gone to aide the people in that war torn country.

The Cluffs are friendly folks who enjoy visiting with any and all who come into their store; they love to share with their guests, local history and tall tales of the old mining days.

The Cardinal Village Resort as it looks today.   SN Photo.

REFERENCES AND NOTES

Interviews with Jim Archer, Hal and Barbara Cluff, Mr. and Mrs. G. G. Kieser, Raymond Milovich, John Schober, Larry Stratton, and David Winkler

CHAPTER
X

THE CARDINAL MINE TODAY

The mine now lies in ruins; each year that passes sees more of the original features gone. All that remains are two wooden structures, several concrete foundations, pieces of wood, metal, canvas, and miscellaneous other remnants of a once thriving operation.

The short walk to the old ruins starts at the Cardinal Lodge, proceeds south between the cabins and on into the woods. After crossing a small stream, the trail continues on some 300 feet where it joins an old

117

road, once used by the miners to get to the mine. After a right turn, the road crosses over Bishop Creek on an old wooden bridge, another remnant of the mining days. Immediately after crossing the bridge, the road, partially covered with a growth of bushes, turns left and follows along the edge of a large mound of tailings, then over a rise and on to the main site of the mining operations.

At the far end of the mound of tailings stands a small wooden building with a metal roof containing an opening for a stove pipe. The age and function of this building are unknown.

Just above the small shed to the southwest, stands the remains of the old Wilshire mill which was a gravity fed operation and consisted of several separate levels. The upper levels (marked by concrete foundations) are the 1912 mill and the lower levels show later additions. The first and uppermost level is where the tramway brought the ore into the mill. A series of 12 by 12 inch timbers anchored in a concrete foundation are present. Nearby lies an iron cog wheel assembly, and further down the slope is a 4 foot metal object with five protrusions which seem to be exhaust ports.

On the second level, a large, raised concrete foundation is all that remains of the stamp mills. Around the foundation are wood planks and timbers, probably remains of the floor. The flotation plant was built on the third level. Part of the concrete foundation remains, with three concrete piers on which two 12 by 12 inch timbers rest. On the down-slope side stand the remains of a rock wall indicating the end of the mill building, shown very clearly in the photograph of the old mill on page 14.

Levels 4 and 5 are believed to be the location of the cyanide plant built in 1914 although nothing remains of the building. These two flat areas, separated

Rock wall and remains of the old Wilshire Mill.   SN Photo.

by a rock wall, show orange to light beige tailings, indicating the use of cyanide in ore processing.

Looking up the canyon toward the southeast, a wooden structure meets the eye. It is the lower portion of the old ore bin/head frame and the most imposing object on the site. Approximately 20 by 20 feet square and standing about 35 feet high, it is tied together with rods and spikes. The head frame structure leans slightly toward the east, crushing part of the concrete foundation and giving it a very unstable appearance. Immediately behind it lie the foundations of the ore bins and behind them, the foundation of the hoist house built in 1933 when the Cardinal Gold Mining Company took over the mine. The upper portion of the hoist house foundation was the location of the actual hoist machinery.

119

On the same level with the base of the head frame and to the east sits a large, mass of concrete, the foundation of a building which had been attached to the head frame and was a part of the hoist operation. Immediately in front of this concrete mass is an adit (an opening into a mine tunnel), blocked off with concrete about five feet into its tunnel.

Adjacent to the ore bin/head frame and to the east is the location of the blacksmith shop. This level 20 by 25 foot area strewn with cinders and fire brick, contains what appears to be a heating element, about 9 feet in length and consisting of eight heating coils. Also located in the blacksmith shop area is a large metal container, about two feet wide, five feet long and three feet high, possibly some sort of fire box.

Head frame with foundations of   (Looking uphill).   SN Photo.
the ore bins behind and the cap magazine
building foundation on its right. An adit in the foreground.

Looking downhill toward Bishop Creek from behind   SN Photo.
the ore bin/head frame, the foundations of the
Cardinal Mill lay beyond and to the left

Located adjacent to Bishop Creek and just beyond the blacksmith shop, is the building depicted on the 1920 map on page 61 as "Compressor House #2." Built in 1909, a 30 by 67 foot, weathered, concrete foundation and several badly deteriorated piers with anchor bolts are all that remain of the building.

Toward the stream and southwest of the head-frame, on a lower level, are the foundations of the Cardinal mill, built in 1934 by the Cardinal Gold Mining Company. An extensive concrete foundation, about 110 feet in width and 120 feet in length remains. Within this foundation are many concrete walls, piers, pipes, and wood beams of various sizes and orientations. Other items within the foundation are a long, wooden stairway and a heavy, iron pulley wheel. Other items present in the area are a cyanide barrel, parts of two wheelbarrows and remnants of an ore cart.

Located to the northwest of the ore bin/head frame on the hillside, sits an adit which was referred to as the Powder Tunnel. It is wood framed and leans rather precariously to the left. Roof fall and debris that blocks off the tunnel holds shut a dilapidated wooden door. Peeking in, one can see that the tunnel appears to be clear for a some distance behind the door. An old map shows an adit in the approximate location of the powder tunnel named the Hassan Tunnel. If they are indeed the same tunnel, it could be assumed the adit was used by both the Wilshire and the Cardinal mining companies.

Entrance to the Powder Tunnel and probably also the Hassan Tunnel.

SN Photo.

Farther up the hillside, between the ore bin/head frame and the old Wilshire mill the adit of the Sanford Tunnel sits next to a sizable area of tailings. This

Entrance to the Sanford Tunnel.   SN Photo.

tunnel was the primary focus of interest during the Cardinal era. A unique feature of this adit is that it is built mostly of round rather than rectangular timbers. A hinged door covers the entrance some 6 to 8 feet into the tunnel and the framing has partially collapsed.

In Bishop Creek alongside the mill and compressor areas are indications that a once active mine used the creek for its operation. Two barrels and several pieces of lumber lie in the creek, and a length of pipe protrudes from the bank out over the water. At one time, too, a bridge existed in this area, however, nothing remains of that bridge today.

Activity also took place on the east side of the creek, as indicated on the 1920s map. At one time, a house, an assay office, and a change house sat on this location. A 22 by 28 foot, concrete foundation, a rock wall, several timbers and fire bricks, some corrugated tin, and an old wooden door are all that remains. There are still indications of a road leading up to that area.

Many other structures once located in the mine area have disappeared entirely, gone without a trace of evidence they ever existed. Their only proof of existence shows in the old photographs that remain, and lies in the memories of those who worked and lived in the area.

Heating element near blacksmith shop.　　　　SN Photo.

REFERENCES AND NOTES

Interviews with Jerry and Nancy Owens, Art and Lou Schober, John Schober, and Mr. and Mrs. Ken Stroman.

U. S. Forest Service.

CHAPTER
XI

ASPENDELL

About a quarter mile down the road from Cardinal Village Resort and eighteen miles southwest of Bishop on State Highway 168, sits the peaceful little settlement of "Aspendell," named for the stands of beautiful aspen trees that grace the valley. Aspendell, surrounded on three sides by majestic mountains, is located on the Middle Fork of Bishop Creek at an elevation of about 8,500 feet.

During the Bishop Creek/Cardinal mining days, Aspendell did not exist. Life centered at the mine village, although, in the 1930s, miners built a few homes in the Aspendell area.

125

During the early 1920s, Mr. Tobe Way, seeing the need for more transportation of supplies in this isolated area, started a pack station on the creek in the heart of the present Aspendell site. In about 1928, teamster and freighter R. J. Schober (father of John and Art Schober of Bishop), took over the pack station and moved it from the creek to a location in the northwest part of Aspendell at the foot of the mountains. The Schober brothers ran the pack station (commonly known as the Pack Shack) for many years. Upon completion of a road to North Lake, the Schobers built another pack station in that area. The old home site in Aspendell, with its corrals and out-buildings, still remain in use today. Management of the station changed hands again in 1994 when the Schobers sold it to Mike Morgan of the Bishop Pack Outfitters.

Around 1961, Gene Scherer of the Sierra Development Co. of Long Beach paid a visit to the area now known as Aspendell and immediately fell in love with the place. He had a dream that someday, he could make this virgin and beautiful land available for others to enjoy and live in.

He purchased 120 acres and started developing the project, first called "Sierra Estates," using his own money along with money from other investors. He laid out a tract with all utilities underground and all sewage in a central system. One of the investors, Dick Aldcroft, suggested the name "Aspendell" which they adopted. Eugene Sherer's dream was about to come true.

Previous to December 1961, the Cardinal Village and the Schober Pack Station obtained their water from the creek. On December 19, 1961, the California Secretary of State granted articles of incorporation to Gene Scherer who established the Aspendell Mutual Water Company. F. J. Scherer, Charles Scherer, Jr., and

Gordon Holmes served as its first directors. In July 1969, Scherer turned the water company over to Aspendell residents. This water company serves Tracts 1 and 3. In about 1979, another water company was formed, the Alpine Water Company, serving Tract 2.

Soon after establishing the water company, Gene Scherer began construction. Contractors built several "spec" homes to speculate how sales would go, among them the Wilson, Newlove, and Turner homes. (Turner's house burned in late 1980).

For awhile, the Water Company was the only group representing the Aspendell property owners. Mr. and Mrs. Jim Archer began to see a need for a separate independent entity to better represent the owners in important decisions. So they established the APOA, the Aspendell Property Owners Association. This continues to be a well-organized and important organization to the property owners of Aspendell.

As each lot sold, the APOA by-laws required the association to issue a "Registration of Stock" certificate to the buyer. The first certificate was issued in December 1962, to Sherman Stein, lot number 1-64. The Steins still own the property today.

By 1964, a few new owners built homes along the creek; little by little, Aspendell began to grow. The first year-round resident was Claud Gitchell, 1967, followed by Jim and Lois Archer who established residency in 1970. (Jim Archer is affectionately known as "Aspendell's Mayor.") By 1974. the Aldcrofts, Mitchells, Peters and Turners joined them in full-time life in Aspendell.

The Aspendell Mutual Water Company erected a fire house and formed an operating volunteer fire department. In July 1972, they acquired a "new" used fire truck from the Gulf Oil Company Research Center in La Jolla. Jim and Lois Archer drove the truck home from La Jolla to Aspendell. In the spring of 1981, Aspendell received another "new" fire truck from the Division of Forestry. In 1991, this truck was replaced by a bright red Engine No. 1, purchased from the Bishop Volunteer Fire Department for the sum of $1.00. Later that year, the water company built an addition onto the fire house.

Along side the fire house stands a flag pole, erected and dedicated in July of 1976 by the residents of Aspendell, to celebrate the Bicentennial.

Local residents are justly proud of their "Fire Department," their first line of defense against home fires. The fire department in Bishop does respond in case of a fire but there is quite a delay time in climbing the eighteen mile grade. In the meantime, the Aspendell fire department, manned by a volunteer fire crew, does a tremendous amount of good in holding down fires and keeping them from spreading to adjacent homes.

Aspendell fire trucks got a new look with a coat of the new "Aspen green" paint. Local residents proudly unveiled them on July 3, 1982. Cal and Mary Turner donated the funds for the painting in gratitude for the fire company's aid during their house fire in November, 1980.

Wildlife abounds in the Aspendell and Cardinal Resort areas. Over the years, more than 20 species of mammals and about 75 bird species have been sighted. In summer, mule deer are common, especially mornings and evenings when they go down to the creek to drink. Other animals seen often include the Sierra Chickaree or Douglas' tree squirrel; two kinds of ground squirrels, the Golden Mantled and Belding; chipmunks and white-footed deer mice. Ringtails, relatives of the raccoon and sometimes called miner's cats, are present but very rarely seen as they are nocturnal and very shy. Other mammals living in the area are both striped and spotted skunks, coyotes, raccoons, marmots, and two species of rabbits (one, the black-tailed, turns white in winter). Three types of foxes live in the area, although the red fox and kit fox reportedly have never been seen by residents; the gray fox, however, is fairly common. Several smaller mammals also make their residence in Aspendell. On occasion, bears and mountain lions (also called cougars or pumas) have wandered into the area, causing some excitement among the residents.

Common birds are the raucous Steller's jay, Clark's nutcracker, robin, water ouzel (American Dipper), raven, three or four kinds of woodpeckers, and the house wren, the most vocal of all the birds. Occasionally a majestic red-tailed hawk circles over the area looking for prey. Golden eagles have been observed nesting in the crags above Cardinal Village. The gray-crowned rosy finch, seen virtually nowhere else, brings avid bird-watchers to Aspendell just to see them. Many other birds show up at various times of the year.

Although the Bishop Creek canyon is on the border of the Western Rattlesnake's range, no one has ever seen one in the area. And there are very few non-poisonous snakes. Occasionally a small, harmless garter or water snake may be seen near the creek. Other creatures are frogs and small, charcoal colored lizards.

At times, weather and mother nature have not been kind to Aspendell residents. According to records kept by the Edison Company, the winter of 1968-69 was the worst in the history of the area; January and February received an enormous amount of snow. In February, an avalanche came down through the south eastern part of Aspendell pushing the Olson's cabin completely across Sage Street. On February 17, 1986, history repeated itself when another avalanche swept through the same area, totally destroying the home of Mr. and Mrs. Knapp at 144 Alpine Drive. It also damaged several other homes.

Bishop Creek has flooded over its banks several times when spring snow melt fills the Sabrina Dam and causes it to flow over the spillway. The worst flooding, however, occurred on September 26, 1982, when the North Lake dam broke, causing Bishop Creek to flood over its banks. The water also inundated parts of Bishop.

North Lake is a natural lake. In the early 1900s, the power company built a small dam downstream from the lake, creating a small shallow lake on the outlet stream. In time, the small lake backed up to the natural lake. When an excessive amount of water was received, the water level in the entire lake area rose. In September 1982, the dam was unable to withstand the pressure of the above normal water level caused by heavy rains and snow melt from a sudden, tropical storm. The dam burst, sending the excessive water surging down Bishop Creek toward the city of Bishop. (This left North Lake's natural lake, full). No one reported injuries, but damage amounted to approximately $7.5 million.

Bob Wallace of Aspendell observed the water coming down the mountainside from North Lake, shortly before the dam broke. He concluded by the amount and color of the water that the dam was failing. "There was quite a gully going," Wallace said. "It looked like 30 to 50 feet deep. The darn water was just a brown spray all over the place, over the top of the gully. I drove back down to the road and told my wife. She called the police department and told them the dam was breaking."

The raging water completely washed out the bridge on Highway 168, near the Bishop Park campground and washed out the road to the campground, leaving the residents of Aspendell and the Cardinal Lodge completely stranded. The water also did minor damage to two homes along the creek.

Life did not get back to normal for several weeks. The power company never rebuilt the North Lake dam, thus doing away with that threat in the future.

Many years ago, Schober's Pack Shack put in the first telephone to be installed in the area. Later the Cardinal Lodge installed a telephone. In 1978, the telephone company made party lines available to Aspendell residents, and in 1985 they received private line service.

There are 160 lots in Aspendell, 104 with homes built on them. At the present time, 1995, about 33 families make Aspendell their year-round home. Many more spend week-ends and vacations relaxing in the restful atmosphere of this picturesque community.

Gene Sherer's dream has come true, probably beyond his greatest expectations. Aspendell will continue to grow and many more fortunate people will have the satisfaction of living in that beautiful area.

REFERENCES AND NOTES

U. S. Geological Survey Topographical map, "Mt. Goddard Quadrangle."

Interviews with Jim Archer, Jerry and Nancy Owens, Art and Lou Schober, John Schober, and Mr. and Mrs. Ken Stroman.

The Cardinal Mine as it appeared
in 1937.

Photo courtesy Laws
Railroad Museum.

A

Abelor Ranch, 89
Akins, R. P., 19
Aldcroft, Dick, 126, 127
Allen, Amos, 17
Allison, Mark, 37, 40
Alpine Water Company, 127
Amos, J. C. B., 53
Amos, Mr., 53
Anaheim, CA, 98
Anderson, Dr. Charles, 51, 74
Andrews Camp, 36
Andrews, Frank, 36
APOA, Aspendell Property Owner's Association, 127
Archer, Jim and Lois, 35, 127
Aremu Gold Mine, 5, 101
Arizona, 42
Aspendell Mutual Water Company, 126, 127
Aspendell, 67, 68, 108, 125-131

B

Baboon cabin, 109
Bailey, Richard B., 41, 42
Barlow Lane, 79
Barstow, CA, 88
Barth, Mr., 25
Beauregard, Arch, 24
Beverly Hills, CA, 100
Big Pine, CA, 2, 24, 48
Bishop Creek, 1-3, 5, 33, 42, 57, 64, 75, 79, 86, 87, 118, 121, 123, 125, 130
Bishop Creek Gold Mining Co., see Bishop Creek Mine
Bishop Creek Milling Co., 6, 20
Bishop Creek Mine, 1-5, 7-10, 17, 18, 20, 21, 24-26, 29, 56, 64-66, 69, 70, 79, 81, 85, 86, 89, 91, 101-103, 105, 125
Bishop Creek Mining District, 2, 37
Bishop Creek/Cardinal Gold Mine, see Cardinal Mine
Bishop Light and Power Company, 85, 90
Bishop Museum and Historical Society, 80
Bishop Pack Outfitters, 126
Bishop Volunteer Fire Department, 128

Blue Heaven cabin, 48, 72, 113
Blue Lake cabin, 109
Bodie, CA, 57
Bodle, Ward, 51
Bolivia, 42, 43
Bongard, Victor, 29
Booth, Mr., 18
Bridgeport, CA, 90
British Guiana, 5, 101
Brown, Bob, 37
Bullpit Park, 89
Bulpitt, Ernest Irl "Ernie", 89, 92
Bush, Harold, 51

C

Cable Hill, 8, 69, 70
Caffery, Harry, 51
Cajon Pass, 88
California Electric Company, Northern Division, 89
California Electric Power Company, 90
CalTrans Project Report, 64, 67
Cambria, CA, 91
Camp Sabrina, 35, 50, 114, 115
Canada, 100
Cardinal Gold Mining Company, see Cardinal Mine
Cardinal Lodge, 109, 117, 130, 131
Cardinal Mine, 1, 26, 29, 30, 32, 37, 39, 41-43, 48, 51, 53, 56,
        73, 81, 85, 105, 111, 119, 121
Cardinal Mine, diagram of, 40
Cardinal Village Resort, 57, 107-109, 111, 112, 115, 116, 125
Cardinals, 48
Carlyle, Albert "Sailor", 34
Carlyle, Laura, 34
Carson and Colorado Railroad Company, 77, 79
Carson City, NV, 77
CCC boys, 48
Central Park, 101
Cerro Gordo Mine, 2
Challenge Magazine, 100
Chidago District, 37, 51
Cholome, CA, 74
Clark Williams Hospital, 71, 73

Clark, J. W., Postmaster, 18, 103
Cleland, Carl, 73
Cleland, Deston "Duke", 37, 51, 73
Cleland, Sam, 37, 73
Cluff, Hal and Barbara, 107, 108, 115, 116
Coen, Gleason, 79, 89, 90, 91
Coen, Irene, 79, 89
Colorado Iron Works Company, 19
Colorado River, 77
Comstock claim, 5
Consolidated Metals Corp., 25, 26, 29
Consolidated Mining Company, 24
Consolidated Wilshire Mining Company, 22, 103
Consort Mining Company, 2
Cooley, N. J., 88
Corona, CA, 88
Croatia, 116
Curran, H. T., 22
Curtis, Loren, 86

D

Dean, Robert, 51
DeCamp, Val, 29, 41, 42
Dempsey, Jack, 30
Doheney, 98
Dolan, Ted, 22, 23
Domingus, Ralph and Rosie, 35
Dougherty, Dean, 92
Dougherty, Harvey, 91, 92
Dougherty, Louise, 91, 92, 93
Drunken Sailor building, 113
Dugan, John, 88
Dyer, Maxine Skaggs, 31, 48

E

Eck, John, 41, 42
Elks Park, 89
Elliott, Stuart, 22
Elsinore, CA, 88
Emerald cabin, 52, 75, 108
Everett, J. C., 23

I

Ida Mine, 2
Inderrieden, A. J., 29
Intake I, 87
Intake II, 26, 48, 57, 64, 87-89
Inyo County Bank, 18, 25
Inyo County Court House, 2, 25
Inyo County Recorder's Office, 9
Inyo County, 3, 25, 102
Inyokern, CA, 89, 90
Ionaco, 104
IWW, 25

J

Janeway, G. Harold, 29
Johnson, C. E., 88
Johnson, Charles F., 53
Johnson, Governor Hiram W., 66
Jones, J. Denman, 53
Joslin, Arthur, 22, 23
June Lake, CA, 47
Jung, Carl, 102

K

Kearns, S. R., 20
Keeler, CA, 77, 78, 80
Kennedy, Florence, 79
Keough's Hot Springs, 35, 42, 47, 48
Keough, Senator, 74
Kerr, Mark B., 4
Kieser, Mrs. G. G., 112
Kilpatrick estates, 88
Kinney, Ernest, 7, 74, 75
Kinney, George C., 7, 9, 20, 86, 87
Kinney, Yan, 52, 53, 74, 75
Klipstein, H. W., Jr., 25
Knapp, Mr. and Mrs., 129
Knighton, Leuis "Lou", 49, 74
Knighton, Lucille, 49, 50

O

Olds, Elva, 24
Olds, Manny, 24, 25
Olds, Neill, 24
Olson, 129
Orange County, 98
Otey Village, 36, 37, 67, 108
Otey's store, 36, 108
Otey, Jay Selkirk "Kirk", 36, 108
Owen, Hanna, 99, 100
Owen, William C., 98, 99
Owens Lake, 2
Owens River, 78
Owenyo, CA, 78

P

Paiute District, 2
Paiute Indians, 1
Paiute Pass, 64
Pangingi, 48, 49, 50, 112
Pappas, Nick, 51
Pasadena, CA, 98
Pasear garage, 69
Paso Robles, CA, 57
Patterson, Coroner, 51
Paymasters Quarters, 5, 30, 31, 111
Pelton water wheel, 9, 25
Peters, 127
Phelps, Charles, 88
Pine Creek, 57
Pinneo, Percy Herbert "Bert", 50, 51
Plant 1, 87
Plant 2, 64, 87-89, 91, 93
Plant 3, 64, 67, 87, 91-93
Plant 4, 52, 68, 75, 86, 88, 91-93
Plant 5, 75, 87, 93
Plant 6, 87, 92, 93
Pleasant Grove, UT, 33, 71
Pound, Margaret, 31
Powder Tunnel, 122
Proskey, Col. Winfield Scott, 4

R

Randsburg, CA, 89
Red Light claim, 5
Reeve, Alex, 69, 70
Reno, NV, 41
Reynolds, J. M., 51
Reynolds, Mary, 102
Rhyolite, NV, 88
Rialto, CA, 88
Richards, John V., 22
Riley, Jesse, 20
Rising Sun claim, 5, 8
Riverside County, CA, 88
Rockefeller, 99
Rocky Point claim, 5
Rocky Point mill site, 5
Romelia claim, 2
Rose, Merle, 71
Rosenbloom, Slapsy Maxy, 30
Route 76, 67
Ruble, H. A., 23
Russ Mining District, 2
Russell, Clyde, 42

S

Sabrina Basin, 112
Sabrina Dam, 130
Sabrina, Lake, see Lake Sabrina
San Bernardino County, CA, 88
San Carlos Company, 2
Sand Canyon, 64, 65, 75
Sanford Tunnel, 25, 122
San Francisco, CA, 9, 25, 39, 79, 97, 98
Santa Barbara, CA, 104
Santa Monica, CA, 98
Scherer, Charles Jr., 126
Scherer, E. L., 126
Scherer, Gene, 126, 127, 131
Schober Lodge, 36
Schober Pack Station, "Pack Shack", 8, 33, 71, 91, 126, 131

Stowe, Elizabeth "Lisa", 32
Stowe, Herb, 32, 57, 71
Stratton, Larry and Nadine, 108
Stroman, Ken and Avis, 108
Sullivan Machinery Company, 9
Supervisor's house, 114

T

Taft, President William H., 5
Tassawini Gold Mine, 5, 101
Thompson, Juel, 51
Thunder and Lightning cabin, 112, 113
Tip Top claim, 5
Tip Top Mine, 2
Tonopah, NV, 18, 86, 88
Topsy Turvey cabin, 108
Tracts 1, 2, and 3, 127
Travers, Richard H., 29
Tunney, Gene, 30
Turner, Cal and Mary, 127, 128

U

U. S. Post Office Department, 10, 17, 18, 103
Union Mine, 2
United States Smelting, Refining & Mining Company, 32
United Verde Copper Company, 41
Utter, Walter, 70

V

VanLoon, H. A., 51
Victorville, CA, 88
Vonde, Roy, 51

W

Wallace, Bob, 130
Wallerstedt, G. A., 50, 51
Walter, E. W., 19, 20, 22
Walters, 22, 23
Warriner, 22, 23

Warwick, Lady, 99
Way, Tobe, 126
Wedge lodes, 5
Weekly Nationalist Magazine, 99
Wells, H. G., 98
Westinghouse, 104
Weston, A. B., 53
White Mountains, 2, 65, 86
Wilkins claim, 5
Wilkins, G. W., 4
Williams, Elzie, 91
Williams, George, 91
Wilshire Bishop Creek/Cardinal Mine, see Cardinal Mine.
Wilshire Bishop Creek Gold Mine, see Bishop Creek Mine.
Wilshire Boulevard, 100, 105
Wilshire, George and Clara, 97
Wilshire, Henry Gaylord, 4-6, 17-22, 24, 25, 32, 65, 69, 97-
　　　105, 114
Wilshire, Logan, 102, 103, 105, 106
Wilshire, Mary, 103, 105, 106, 114
Wilshire Tract, 100
Wilshire, William, 97, 98
Wilshire's Magazine, 5, 100, 102
Wilson, 127
Winkler, Dr. David, 104-106
Wofford, Grace Matlick, 31
World War I, 20, 103
World's Greatest Mine, 5, 102

Y

Yaney, Justice, 23
Yerington, Hume, 77
YWAM, Youth With a Mission, 116